STEAM in the AIR

STEAM in the AIR

The
Application
of
Steam Power in Aviation
during the
19th and 20th Centuries

Maurice Kelly

Member of the Newcomen Society,
Formerly 2nd Engineer Officer, Royal
Research Service & British Merchant Navy,
Chief Engineer Officer, Marina Mercante de
Republica de Panama

Pen & Sword
AVIATION

First published in Great Britain in 2006 by
Pen & Sword Aviation
an imprint of
Pen & Sword Books Ltd
47 Church Street
Barnsley
South Yorkshire
S70 2AS

ISBN 1 84415 295 2

A CIP catalogue record for this book is available from the British Library.

Typeset in 10/12 Palatino by
Concept, Huddersfield, West Yorkshire

Printed and bound in Great Britain by
CPI UK

Pen & Sword Books Ltd incorporates the Imprints of Pen & Sword Aviation, Pen & Sword Maritime, Pen & Sword Military, Wharncliffe Local History, Pen & Sword Select, Pen & Sword Military Classics and Leo Cooper.

For a complete list of Pen & Sword titles please contact
PEN & SWORD BOOKS LIMITED
47 Church Street, Barnsley, South Yorkshire, S70 2AS, England
E-mail: enquiries@pen-and-sword.co.uk
Website: www.pen-and-sword.co.uk

Contents

Acknowledgements

The author would like to thank the following for their assistance in the preparation of this book:

Den Burchmore of the Airship Trust

Paul Carslake, Editor of *The Engineer* magazine for permission to reproduce line drawings

R.W. Carter, Curator of the Chard Museum, for details of the Stringfellow Collection housed in the museum

Hannah Cameron of Cameron Balloons Ltd, for information on airship technology etc.

Heloise Cates, for setting up the typescript and storing it on disk

Dr M.F.D. Diprose of the University of Sheffield Department of Electronic and Electrical Engineering

Ronald Gardner of the Training Section, Rolls-Royce Aero Engines, Bristol, for information concerning the replica Stringfellow steam aeroplane built by the Apprentices' Association of the Company

K. Hyde, Librarian of the Shuttleworth Collection, for information about the Frost ornithopter and artifacts held at Old Warden

Philip Jarrett, aviation historian, for assistance with details of pioneer aircraft and also for reading the proofs

Nicholas Kelly, for encouragement and assistance

Andrew Nahum, Curator of the Aeronautical section at the Science Museum, South Kensington, for general assistance

Tris Pinkney, proprietor of Bilbys Café, Chard, for details concerning the Rolls-Royce replica Stringfellow aeroplane and engine which are on permanent show there

The late Malcolm Taylor, for general assistance with the newspaper cuttings and entries over the years

Sqn Ldr Michael Townsend, great nephew of Edward Frost, who provided details of his great uncle's work

Ronald Whitehouse, inventor, who gave the writer details of his steam power unit for aeronautical purposes

Thanks are also due to the Patent Office, the British Library, the Bank of England Archive Department, the BBC and the Somerset County Museum.

Introduction

This book studies the use of steam as a method of propulsion in aviation, and the reasons behind the adoption of steam engines to provide lift and motion in the air. There is also information on the remaining artifacts in various museums around the world.

From a historical point of view, the use of steam engines in aviation was a necessity, for at first, during the nineteenth century, this type of power unit was the only source of energy available for the purpose. Some incredible lightweight machines were created by individuals such as John Stringfellow (1799–1883), and by firms like Ahrbecker, Son & Hamken of Stamford Street in London, during that time. Later, the steam engine became the preserve of aviation enthusiasts who were determined to demonstrate that aircraft could be made to fly successfully using external combustion engines (electricity and compressed air were also utilised). One of these enthusiasts was William J. Besler of the Besler Corporation of California, who took off from the San Francisco Bay Airdrome on 20 April 1933 to make a few circuits of the airfield in a Travelair biplane which was fitted with a monotube steam plant of his design. A number of pioneer experimenters put their minds to the problems of flight generally on the boundary of the nineteenth and twentieth centuries and most of these regarded the steam engine as the only real source of power to make their aircraft achieve sustained flight.

CHAPTER ONE

The Early Pioneers

Sir George Cayley

The real progenitor of powered, heavier-than-air flight was an Englishman named Sir George Cayley (1773–1857), a Baronet residing at Brompton Hall in Yorkshire; he was one of the gifted amateurs who became the backbone of a surge into scientific investigation during the 1800s, and he formulated the science of aerodynamics. He was a prolific inventor and during his career, apart from the description of several different varieties of aircraft, he made many developments in other spheres, including the theory of theatre acoustics, the tension wheel, experiments within the resistance of air to cannon shot and specifications for carriages on 'common roads and railways'. His ideas for flying machines encompassed gliders and helicopters as well as dirigible flight. Sir George was the holder of two important patents not related to aerial navigation: 'New Locomotive Apparatus for Propelling Carriages', which described a crawler track mechanism (Brit. Pat. No. 5260 of 1825) and 'Apparatus for Propelling Carriages on Common Roads or Railways' (Brit. Pat. No. 7351 of 1837). Although his invention of the tension wheel, which he sought to apply to aircraft, was possibly the first demonstration of the 'bicycle wheel' principle, he was forestalled by Theodore Jones, who patented the device on 11 October 1826 (Brit. Pat. No. 5415 of 1826).

The invention of the mechanical prime mover in the eighteenth century by Thomas Newcomen kick-started the industrial revolution and gave a fillip to others to develop other forms of apparatus to produce manufactured items or systems of transport. The early part of the nineteenth century saw a rash of patented mechanisms, ranging from velocipedes such as the 'pedestrian curricle' invented by Denis Johnson (Brit. Pat. No. 4321 of 1818) to the fantastic 'aerial steam carriage' of William Samuel Henson (1805–1888) who filed his application in 1842 (Brit. Pat. No. 9478 of 1843). Cayley made his initial foray into the realms of aeronautical science in 1792 when he constructed a model helicopter that was similar in design to one that had been flown successfully in France by Launoy and Bienvenu in 1784; this appliance was simple, for it consisted of two banks of four feathers inserted into corks in a cruciform pattern, and was actuated by a bow and drawstring power system. This helicopter had contra-rotating blades top and bottom and was, as initially built in France, unique. However, it seems to have been based upon an ancient design which had been made as a children's toy for centuries and which consisted of a bamboo tube housing a shaft on which were fixed two blades set at an angle to each other. This blade-and-shaft arrangement was placed into the tube and the shaft was rotated by means of a string; the device then rose into the air. This system could have originated in the Orient; the writer has one that was purchased in a corner shop in Bath during the Second World War.

In 1799 Cayley engraved some designs on a silver disc which depicted the forces acting on a plane surface on the obverse side and had a sketch of a proper aeroplane on the reverse side; this disc is now deposited in the National Collection at the Science Museum in South Kensington, London. A few years later, in 1804, he made and flew a model glider which became the first true heavier-than-air machine to achieve a controlled flight, and was probably inspired by the engraving on the silver disc. Also in 1804 he made his most pertinent prophesy when he stated: 'I am convinced that aerial navigation will form a most prominent feature in the progress of civilization'.

It is certain that the writings and inventions of Sir George Cayley inspired pioneers such as Henson and Stringfellow to advance their theories for the 'aerial steam carriage' and it appears that a glider of triplane form that was demonstrated by Cayley in 1849 using a 10-year old boy as a 'passive pilot', influenced the construction of the steam triplane constructed by Stringfellow in 1868. This early glider experiment was not a proper flight for it appears that the machine was tethered during the experiment.

Some details of the aircraft built by Cayley show that his grasp of aeronautics made him to be the real precursor of manned flight; whilst the writer does not in any way wish to denigrate the achievements of Henson and Stringfellow, Clément Ader, the Wright brothers and others, it would appear that the original inventor of the aeroplane was, definitely Sir George Cayley, for his designs, calculations and prophesies have formed the basis of today's aeronautical knowledge and, together with the original work in space travel revealed by the Russian scientist, Konstantin Edouardovich Tsiolkovsky (1857–1935), have made the feats of aerial navigation performed during the twentieth and twenty-first centuries possible.

Sir George Cayley demonstrated three distinct styles of aircraft in his work, of which two would have required a power unit in order to fly. The first type was the glider, of which two were actually made in full-sized form; both were probably triplanes, one was the triplane of 1849, mentioned earlier, and the other a man-carrying machine which took Sir George's coachman across a valley on the Brompton Hall Estate in the early 1850s. Drawings for a further, monoplane version were published in the *Mechanics Magazine* of 25 September 1852 (see fig. 1). This second flight was witnessed by Sir George's grand-daughter, Mrs George Thompson, who wrote the following account of the spectacle in 1921:

> *I have scratched my memory as to the date of his flying machine which I saw fly across the dale. It was in 1852 or 1853. Everyone was out on the east*

Figure 1. A drawing of a monoplane, man-carrying glider designed by Sir George Cayley in about 1852 and illustrated in *Mechanics Magazine* on 25 September 1852. It was never built.

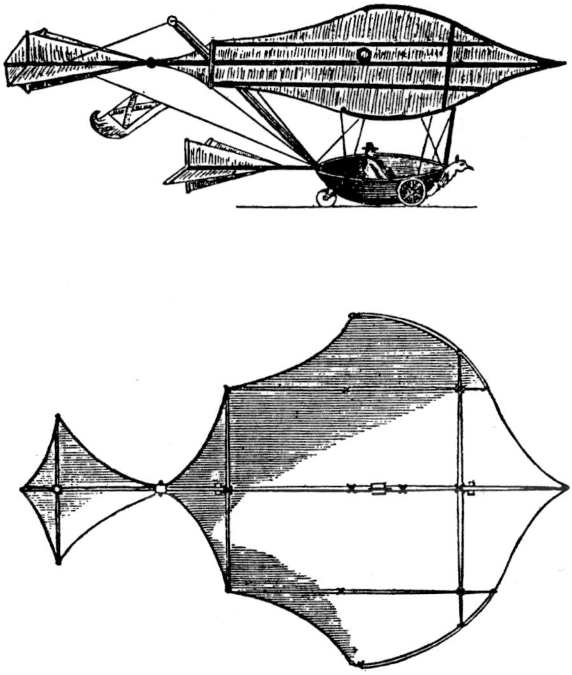

side and saw the start from close to. The coachman went in the machine and landed on the west side about the same level. I think it came down rather a shorter distance than expected. The coachman got himself clear, and when the watchers had got across he shouted, 'Please Sir George. I wish to give notice. I was hired to drive and not to fly.' That's all I recollect. The machine was put away in the barn, and I used to sit and hide in it from my Governess when so inspired'.

The veracity of this account has never been challenged and, although it seems singular, there appears to be no reason to doubt it even after eighty years.

A dirigible propelled by a steam engine was envisaged by Cayley and an illustration of it was published in 1816 (see fig. 2); this airship had two distinct forms of propulsion: one by means of screw propellers and one by flapping wings. Another picture of an airship depicts a dual envelope system joined in the horizontal plane with just a gondola and a triangular 'mizzen' rudder.

Another aircraft proposed by Sir George Cayley was the 'convertiplane' (see fig. 3). This machine was the result of a suggestion made by Robert Taylor in 1842, and was not part of Sir George's original thought; the drawing was published in *Mechanics Magazine* of the 8 April 1843 and it indicated the current understanding of the need for contra-rotating rotor blades; the design is remarkable for its period in that similar machines were constructed in the twentieth century by Paul Cornu and Etienne Oemiched in France, Professor Focke in Germany, and Ivan Bratukhin in the Soviet Union.

Regarding the use of prime movers for aeronautical purposes, Cayley investigated the use of hot air and steam as agents and even proposed a form of internal combustion engine. Having invented an 'expansion air engine' (i.e. a hot-air engine), in 1805 he went on to build a model 'gunpowder' engine. He also described a steam engine for aeronautical use in 1807 and this unit was probably envisaged as propulsion for the dirigible that was later described in 1816. The engine was a single-cylinder, 1 hp machine that had a theoretical weight of 163 lb. It was to be fired with coal and its fuel consumption was rated at 5½ lb per hp. In 1809 he made this statement concerning the future of aviation and the need for an effective power unit to seal that future:

I feel perfectly confident, however, this noble art will soon be brought home to man's general convenience, and that we shall be able to transport ourselves and families, and their goods and chattels, more securely by air than by water, and with a velocity of from 20 to 100 miles per hour. To produce this effect it is only necessary to have a first mover, which will

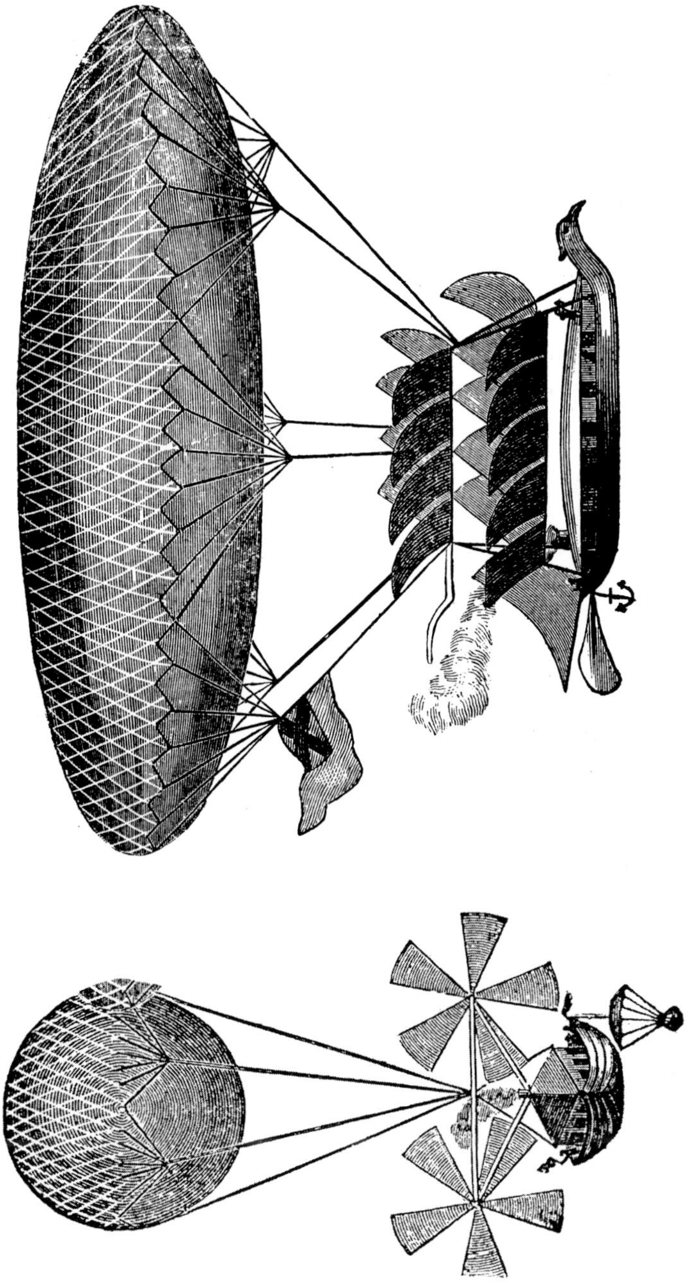

Figure 2. The dirigible proposed by Sir George Cayley. The airship was obviously designed to use steam for propulsion and two methods of motion are illustrated: twin fan-like airscrews or two banks of flapping wings. Items of note are the hanging parachute, the boiler/engine house in the boat-style gondola and the anchor. Another design which was similar to the above sketch showed a dual envelope system joined together in the horizontal plane. This airship was described in 1816.

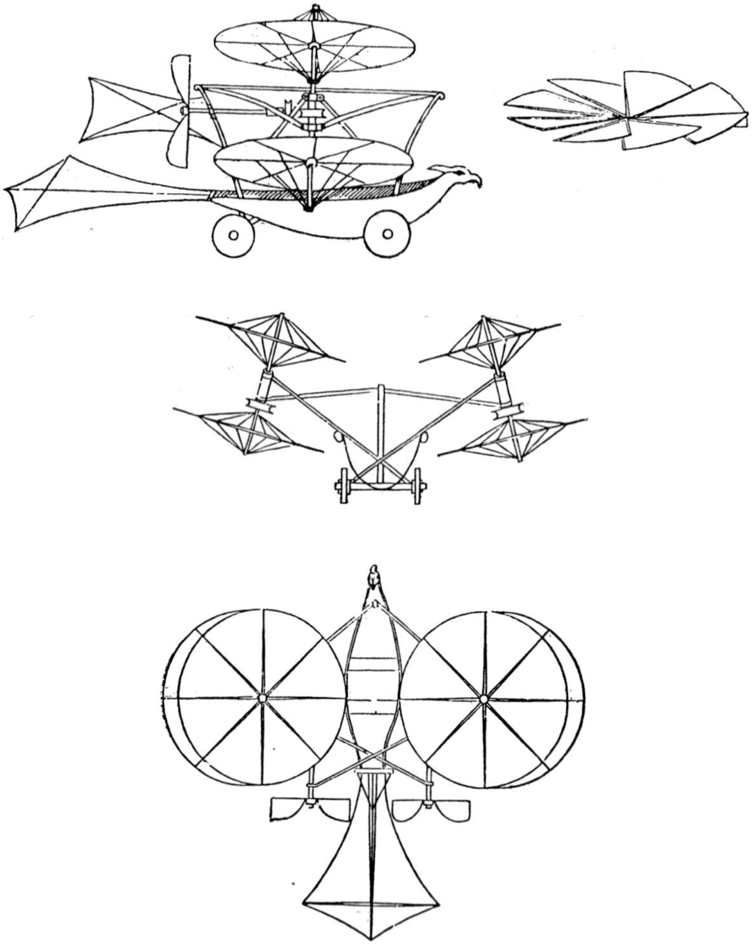

Figure 3. The helicopter design that was proposed by Sir George Cayley in 1843. This drawing was published in *Mechanics Magazine* on Saturday, 8 April 1843.

generate more power in a given time, in proportion to its weight, than the animal system of muscles.

Again, between 1809 and 1810, he said:

It may seem superfluous to enquire further relative to a first mover for aerial navigation but lightness is of so much value in this instance that it is proper to notice the probability that exists using the expansion of air by the sudden combustion of inflammable powders or fluids, with great advantage. Probably a much cheaper engine of this sort might be produced by a gas-tight apparatus and by firing the inflammable air with a due portion of common air under the piston.

He also had a vision of jet propulsion using a steam engine when he made this statement:

> *Communicating centrifugal force to air using a hollow drum and fans by the steam engine, is another means of getting propelling power conveniently applicable in every direction that may be required; for by having a movable mouthpiece, from which the air escapes, the reaction will always be in the opposite direction.* [i.e. from every action there will be an equal and opposite reaction, which is the basis of modern jet engine technology, together with the moveable jets which are used today in 'jump-jet' systems.]

He made another pertinent observation concerning helicopter rotor blades when, in 1843, he noted: 'When the engine power is applied, to make them revolve in their proper directions, one set adverse to the other.' Cayley also knew that by setting rotors at angles the power of ascent or descent could be regulated, especially when used in conjunction with a hinged tailplane.

When Sir George died on 15 December 1857 at his home in Yorkshire, he had laid all the theoretical foundations for powered flight in the spheres of both aerostats and aerodynes. With aerostats he lived to see the fruition of his ideas when Henri Giffard made his successful flight in a powered dirigible in 1852, but with heavier-than-air craft, the parameters that he laid down were largely ignored by those who followed him, and much of his work was redone, unnecessarily, in the late nineteenth century.

To sum up the life and times of Sir George Cayley it is only necessary to record his more important achievements: his investigations into the various branches of technical science, his exhaustive revelations concerning aeronautics, and his quest for a lightweight prime mover. He was probably the first scientist to utilize the 'whirling arm' in experiments into aeronautics. This device had been invented by Elliot and Robins in 1746 for use in ballistic tests and Cayley took it up in tests for lift and drag in plane surfaces; he built three of them, one in 1804, another in 1818 and the final one in 1850. The 'whirling arm' was used later, in the final decade of the nineteenth century, by both Professor Samuel Pierpoint Langley in the USA and Sir Hiram Maxim in England; today it is an essential environmental testing machine in the aerospace industry. From this it can be seen that in the sphere of theoretical science, Cayley was as much a 'giant' as was Isambard Kingdom Brunel in the practical areas of technology.

Apart from his legacy in the aeronautical field, Sir George had many other interests; he was a poet, he ran an effective and prosperous country estate, and he was, for a short time, the Whig member of parliament for the town of Scarborough. Also within his lifetime he was to initiate technical education by founding the Regent Street Polytechnic in London in 1839.

Sir William Congreve (1772–1828)

Congreve was a colonel in the army who developed the science of rocketry for use in war. He worked at the Royal Laboratory and at Woolwich Arsenal. His claim to fame is that he demonstrated iron-cased powder rockets successfully at the Arsenal in 1804 and 1805, and these were used with some success during the Napoleonic Wars in 1806 and 1807 at Bologne and Copenhagen. They were also used later in America, and had a fearsome effect when the British attacked Fort McHenry in Baltimore on 13 and 14 September 1814. He went on to improve these rockets and sealed a patent for them in 1823 (Brit. Pat. No. 4853 of 1823); he was knighted for his efforts in this field.

In 1828 Sir William declared his interest in aeronautics when he wrote: 'I shall proceed to develop a plan for raising the human body in the air by a Rotative motion, which ... I think will be more likely to produce a successful result than anything yet attempted.' He went on to describe an aircraft fitted with four rotary propellers furnished with eight vanes of silk stretched over tubular frames made from brass; these were to be manoeuvred by means of a form of collective-pitch control system. He went on to state that if one of his flying machines was to be propelled by steam (he also had ideas for manual propulsion), it would only need a power unit of 3 hp to drive twenty-four propellers each 12 ft in diameter! His calculations seem to be bizarre for it was recorded that the forward motion would be 73 ft per second, with a lift of 840 lb. His figures revealed that the weight of the engine and boiler would be 2,000 lb and the weight of fuel 1,500 lb. He would also need 500 lb of feed-water. The weight of the airframe would be 2,400 lb, a four-man crew would weigh 600 lb, leaving 1,400 lb as an effective pay-load. He also estimated that nine or ten men could use the disposable pay-load and that they could be transported 1,200 miles per day for a week. Sir William's steam helicopter would therefore be able to fly for 8,400 miles at a rate of about 50 mph, consume fuel at 5.6 lb per mile, to lift 3¾ tons into the air, all on 0.8 hp per ton! Nevertheless, his ideas were published in issue No. 240 of the *Mechanics Magazine* for

22 March 1828, where a drawing representing the aircraft was shown together with explanations of its characteristics and potential effectiveness. This fanciful apparatus was never proceeded with, as Congreve died a few weeks after the publication of the article.

Vittorio Sarti

An early proposal for rotating wing flight was made in 1828 by an Italian, Vittorio Sarti with his 'aero veliero' which had a pair of contra-rotating rotors consisting of sails mounted co-axially and which were driven by jets of steam emanating from a boiler mounted at the base of the rotor shaft (see fig. 4). This machine was a conjectural idea and the writer assumes that is was never built.

F.D. Artingstall

Artingstall is known to have built and flown a model ornithopter in 1829 and 1830. He made a two-wing, full-sized machine at first, which he suspended from the ceiling for a test run; this device was driven by a steam engine and, on test, it eventually flapped itself to pieces, after which the boiler exploded! A second version was constructed, with four wings this time, beating alternately; the same fate befell this effort.

The Early Attempts of William Samuel Henson and John Stringfellow

It was the collaboration between Henson and Stringfellow which gave the world some hope for powered heavier-than-air flight. It would appear that Henson was the theorist and that Stringfellow was the engineer, though the former, to give him his due, had produced engineering items himself. Henson hailed from Nottingham and was apprenticed in the lace trade; he was also a skilled machinist and an inventor of note, filing a patent for the manufacture of ornamental lace in 1835 before sealing his now famous patent describing the 'Locomotive Apparatus for the Air, Land and Water' (Brit. Pat. No. 9478 of 1842). He had moved to Chard in Somerset in the early 1830s, where he set up business as W.S. Henson Lace Manufacturer.

John Stringfellow was the son of a Sheffield cutler and he was born at Townwell Yard, Attercliffe on 6 December 1799. In 1815 he was apprenticed to a bobbin-net lace maker in Nottingham and in 1819 he was sent to Chard to install machinery in a factory in Mill Lane. Soon after this he set up in business in the Somerset town as a bobbin and carriage maker. He became influential in Chard; he was a Liberal councillor, was involved in the introduction of street lighting and, in 1839, was instrumental in founding the Chard Institute, a scientific body which held weekly lectures and had a distinguished local membership. Amongst his achievements were patents for medical batteries, a mobile shield for riflemen and blood-letting instrumentation. He was also a skilled taxidermist, an ornithologist and a pioneer of photography.

It was a quirk of fate that these two aeronautical pioneers ended up in the same small Somerset town, but their meeting put Chard on the map of aviation for all time. By 1840 they were engrossed in the experiments to achieve heavier-than-air flight. As Sir George Cayley had pointed out, there was a need for a lightweight power unit to make this dream viable. They planned a large aeroplane and recruited a character named John Bondfield to shoot different birds to provide specimens for the study of flight. The proposed aeroplane was to be a high-aspect-ratio monoplane with a controllable empennage and rudder and was to be fitted with 10 ft diameter pusher airscrews driven by a steam engine that developed between 24 and 30 hp. Again it was the provision of a suitable engine that proved to be a stumbling block and Henson searched everywhere for a machine that was capable of doing the job.

Henson left Chard in 1840 to assist his father in London but this did not hinder the work, for experiments in construction of both airframes and engines continued both there and in Chard. A series of models were tested down a form of slipway and Stringfellow busied himself with producing engines and boilers. By 1842, although true flight had not yet been achieved, there was a need to protect the invention and the patent was filed and provisionally accepted in that year. Encouraged by the acceptance of the invention, Henson launched the first airline, the Aerial Transit Company with two partners, Frederick Marriot, a journalist and a resident of Chard, and D.E. Columbine who was an attorney at law. The purpose of this collaboration was to exploit Henson's patent and to place it upon a commercial footing, with the partners fulfilling diverse roles. Marriot, who was friendly with a member of parliament was to exert influence, Henson and Stringfellow were both responsible for the technical side of the association and Columbine was to act as secretary to the company and to attend to legal matters.

Marriot was successful in gaining influence, for he induced J.A. Roebuck, the MP for Bath, to make an application to procure incorporation under an Act of Parliament whilst Columbine drew up a prospectus to appeal for funds to secure the patent. This prospectus was couched in extravagant terms, extolling the virtues of aerial travel and its vast possibilities. Its proposal read as follows:

For subscriptions of sums of £100, in furtherance of an Extraordinary Invention, not at present safe to be developed, by securing the necessary Patents, for which three times the sum advanced, namely £300, is conditionally guaranteed for each subscription on February 1st. 1844, in case of the anticipations being realized, with the option of the subscribers being shareholders for the large amount, if so desired, but not otherwise.

J.A. Roebuck moved for leave to introduce a Bill providing for an Act of Parliament for incorporation for the Aerial Transit Company on 24 March 1843. This motion was agreed and the Bill was read 'amidst much laughter'. The request for funding in the original prospectus did not meet with any great response, though the sealing of the patent on 26 March and the publicity campaign instigated by Columbine did create interest in the press and aroused public interest for a short time. Details of the 'new wonder' appeared in *Mechanics Magazine* on 1 April 1843 in a paper written by 'L.L.', and in *The Times* on 30 March, where the scheme was described as being 'of very scientific conception, carefully and perseveringly wrought out'. Caricature followed, with *Punch* to the fore, talking about the 'aerial steam carriage's' possible journeys 'from the top of the Monument in Fish Street Hill every morning and taking five minutes to the summit of the Great Pyramid'. Vivid imagination took over with artistic prints appearing depicting the vehicle at various locations in London, in India etc. Eventually, however, serious discussion turned to ridicule and one illustration showed the carriage with engine failure in mid-air when the boiler exploded!

In the aftermath of the publicity for the Aerial Transit Company, Henson conducted further experiments with clockwork-powered models, which seemed to be unsuccessful, and one with a small steam engine, but it was all abortive and finally he proposed that the interests of both Marriot and Columbine be bought out of the patent. This was done, for, following a letter of 18 November 1843, Henson joined Stringfellow at Chard the following December and they agreed 'to construct a model of an Aerial Machine to be employed in such a manner as the parties named above shall consider best and most profitable'. Both Marriot and Columbine faded from the picture and the Aerial Transit Company receded into oblivion as the whole scheme was discredited. However, this was not the end of the story for they both went on to build and demonstrate effective, flying machines which have justly made them famous in the realms of aeronautics.

Chapter Two

The Era of Successful Flight

Henson's and Stringfellow's later Work

It would be fair to say that with the collaboration of Henson and Stringfellow the era of powered flight dawned, for the original designs of William Henson followed the parameters laid down by Sir George Cayley. However, whilst most sources have indicated that there was a close association between the two men there has been no direct evidence that John Stringfellow ever took any part in the design of the patent specification of 1842. It would seem that the whole of the original project was formulated in haste and the introduction of a company to promote aerial steam navigation so soon after the publication of the patent, but without even a model prototype being produced, laid the project open to ridicule and hampered serious scientific investigations into heavier-than-air flight. Perhaps Henson was so taken with the possibilities of his machine that he was, in his own mind, assured of success without adequately thinking out a plan of action which would have included a process of serious development. In all probability, Henson was in need of finance to continue his research and this factor caused him to embark on premature publicity. But whatever the causes of the failure of the Aerial Transit Company the result of the speculation was that the scheme was discredited in the eyes of the general public.

Nevertheless, it is on record that Henson joined Stringfellow at Chard in December 1843 and that they commenced building a prototype which consisted of a small model 'operated by a spring', presumably by clockwork. A larger machine was considered, with a wingspan of 20 ft, and this was made in the form of the 'aerial steam carriage' (see page 2 colour section), which in turn was based upon the drawing found in the 1842 patent specification (see page 3 colour section). The construction of these models was the outcome of a proper agreement between the two partners, as indicated in Chapter 1.

The small model that was produced was apparently unsuccessful, but the second machine was the result of careful thought over a period of three years, from 1844 to 1847. This aeroplane had all the elements that were to be found in a modern design, for it had a fuselage upon which were mounted the wings, a proper tailplane and rudder, two pusher airscrews powered by a steam engine contained in the body of the aircraft, and was fitted with a tricycle undercarriage. On either wing a system of bracing wires was used with king-posts above and below each plane; the king-posts were made of a 'streamline' section and the actual bracing was by flat steel wire which presented minimal drag in the direction of flight. This system of rigging was devised by Henson and the planes themselves were braced internally using piano wire inserted diagonally between the upper and lower surfaces. These surfaces were built up on three longitudinal spars to which were fitted cambered ribs covered with oiled silk. The wings were attached to the power car by means of metal sockets and were easily removable for maintenance. The fan-shaped tailplane was made from a single fabric-covered surface supported by five radially disposed members, whilst beneath it was a small triangular rudder to be used for steering. The tailplane had controls to raise it upwards or downwards in order to provide ascent or descent at will.

In all probability the power unit was the work of Stringfellow alone and it was possibly the first purpose-made aero engine in the world; considerable time and effort was employed in perfecting it; all manner of cams, tappets and eccentrics were tried to actuate the slide valve to obtain optimum results. The piston rod passed through the cylinder covers and the connecting rods worked directly on the propeller shaft crank. The two airscrews were left- and right-handed and were contra-rotating; they were 3 ft in diameter with four blades which took up 75 per cent of the circumference and were set at an angle of 60 degrees. At the original trials compressed air was used but this form of power was soon abandoned in favour of steam and on one of the first tests under power the following notes were made on 27 June 1845:

> *Boiler filled with 50 oz water, burner filled with 10 oz spirit and lighted at 08.45 hrs and steam raised to 100 psi two minutes later when the engine was started. It worked successfully for nine minutes making a total of 2,288 revolutions or 254 rpm. The engine did not prime and 40 oz of the water was consumed during the trial to make 57 revs to the oz. Propeller thrust was measured at 5 lb 4½ oz at the outset settling down to 4 lb ½ oz during the*

run which was conducted at one-third cut-off throughout. The engine had a bore of 1½ in and a stroke of 3 in.

The whole machine was tested initially down inclined wide rails but these tests were inconclusive and thereafter Stringfellow decided to conduct proper flight trials out in the open air. In 1847 a tent was erected at Bala Down, some 2 miles from Chard, and the machine was taken there at night by Stringfellow and two workmen. Unfortunately these trials were unsuccessful; the machine failed to sustain itself, for when it was launched into the air it descended in a gradual glide. The calculations made at the time showed that the thrust was quite able to power the aircraft, being around 5 lb, and the plane area of 70 sq. ft being adequate to support a weight of less than 30 lb. It was the speed of propulsion that was lacking. Other problems were also evident at these trials; as they were conducted at night, the effect of dew on the fabric created problems and the conditions of eddy in the wind proved to be disastrous. However, the engine performed in an exemplary fashion.

After seven weeks of experiment culminating in the failure to achieve sustained flight Henson, who was also in financial difficulties, faded out of the picture. He had applied to Sir George Cayley for support on 28 September 1846, telling him of his co-operation with Stringfellow and suggesting that Cayley's air engine might be used. Sir George had replied that if Henson could show proof of sustainable flight using mechanical power he might be interested but as he did not really have the capital needed at that time, he could not help in that direction. In any case he said that balloon aerial navigation could be 'done readily' and, of course, he was right.

John Stringfellow was also in need of money, and applied to the largest employer in Chard, a lace-maker named John Gifford, only to be told 'to give up this nonsense, God never meant man to fly and we shall never fly'! Henson left Chard in 1848 and married before emigrating to the USA where he died in 1888.

The 1844–47 craft had a wingspan of 20 ft and a parallel chord of 3½ ft to give a wing area of 70 sq. ft; the tailplane area was 10 sq. ft and the all-up weight with the engine fitted was stated to be between 25 and 28 lb. Eventually the machine was sent with other artefacts to an exhibition in London in 1903, after which it passed into the hands of C.H. Alderson who in collaboration with P.Y. Alexander restored it to an approximation of its original condition and presented it to the Science Museum in 1907. The engine for this machine is also in the Science Museum for John Stringfellow's son, F.J. Stringfellow, donated it to C.H. Alderson who, in turn gave it to the museum, also in 1907. This engine, which is shown in fig. 9, had been modified in some way on the tail-rods, having originally 'worked both sides, or ends, of the cylinder direct on the propellers'. The boiler and its container were never received by Alderson.

After Henson left the partnership in 1848, John Stringfellow continued with experiments into mechanical flight, labouring alone, in order to persevere with the dream of sustained flight. In that year he attempted flights with a new model, which were demonstrated at Chard and at Cremorne Gardens in London. This third aircraft was constructed in a disused lace factory in Chard in June 1848 and was about half the size of the 'aerial steam carriage'. It had a wingspan of 10 ft and a maximum chord of 2 ft, with the wings tapering to points at their extremities. The length of the tailplane was 3 ft 6 in and it was 22 in across at its widest part. Although the configuration of the machine was different from the previous model it did embody several of the ideas from it predecessor's design, for again it featured left- and right-hand airscrews 16 in in diameter, with four blades each to occupy 75 per cent of the area of the circumference, being set at an angle of 60 degrees. The engine was a double-acting unit with a bore of ¾ in and a stroke of 2 in. A bevel gear on the crankshaft drove the propellers in the ratio of 3:1.

This aeroplane was tested along a wire and it was released in the following way. After steam had been raised and the propellers had attained maximum speed it was launched down the wire, which was inclined slightly downwards. A lower member on the launching apparatus later encountered a block on the wire which was positioned by prior experiment. The machine would then be allowed to take off and to sustain itself in the air. A run of 22 ft seemed to have been the best distance and a sheet of canvas was laid at this point so that if the model launched prematurely it would not be damaged by a swift descent.

The first trials were made in a room of the disused lace factory in Chard, 66 ft long and between 10 and 12 ft high. The inclined wire was set in a low position in order to allow sufficient space for the aeroplane to rise into the air when free flight was achieved. John Stringfellow's son, Frederick, writing in 1892, gave two accounts of experimental 'flights' made with this machine, one at Chard and another in London at Cremorne Gardens. Regarding the Chard experiment, he stated that the wire only occupied one half of the length of the room to allow an area for the machine to clear the floor. At the first attempt, the tailplane or elevator was set at too high an angle and the machine stalled, with the empennage striking the floor and being damaged on impact. Luckily the damage was superficial and was soon repaired in time for a second attempt to be made with reduced tailplane incidence. The aeroplane left the launching wire and rose into the air, only to be restrained by a special canvas break set some yards away. It was recorded at the time that the machine had achieved a rise of 1 in 7 and had gone a distance of 40 ft in powered free flight. It was later said that when these trials were in progress at least three persons witnessed the events: J. Rist, a prominent Chard lace manufacturer, Northcote Spicer Esq., and J. Toms Esq. However, when this account was written two of the witnesses had died, so perhaps the authenticity of the 'flight' could have been in doubt. Today, moreover, most modern authors are inclined to state that as it was neither sustained nor controlled, it did not count as being a true flight in the meaning of the word.

The 1848 Stringfellow monoplane also found its way to the Science Museum; its major components, including the fuselage, wings, tail, propellers and starting carriage were also sent to London in 1903 and eventually passed into the possession of C.H. Alderson who, in conjunction with P.Y. Alexander, presented them to the National Collection in 1908. The original idea was to reassemble the model and display it in a position attached to its starting mechanism in order to present the method of launching, but as the dismantled parts had so deteriorated the idea was dropped. Nevertheless, discussions were held concerning the fate of these parts and eventually, in 1926, a reproduction of the machine was constructed to the same scale, together with a full set of drawings taken from the original relics. After the 1848 experimental flights the engine and boiler were removed from the aeroplane and were installed in the plant of John Heathcoat Amory & Co. of Tiverton, Devon, to drive a lace machine; when it arrived there the two components were seen to be modified, with the bevel gearing absent and the boiler casing changed.

Heathcoat Amory denied making these alterations and it may be assumed that Stringfellow did this himself. Illustrations of the machine and its power plant are to be found in figs 4, 5 and 6. In 1908 this engine and boiler were presented to the Science Museum by their owners.

After the work on the 1848 machine was finished, Stringfellow busied himself with other tasks, and, a year later he visited the USA. Upon his return to Chard he did not involve himself with any more aeronautical experiments; it was to be fifteen years before he made another attempt with flying machines when the founding of the Aeronautical Society of Great Britain in 1866 aroused his interest once more. At the first meeting of the society on 27 June 1866 Francis

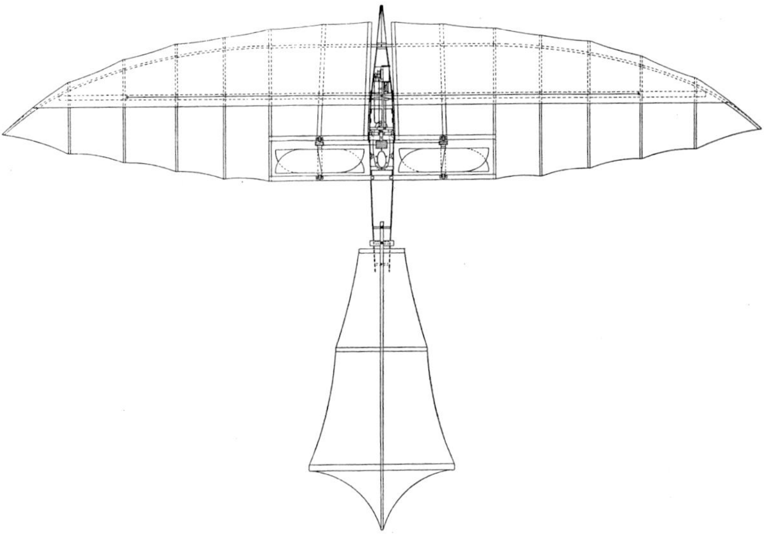

Figure 4. Plan view of the Stringfellow monoplane of 1848.

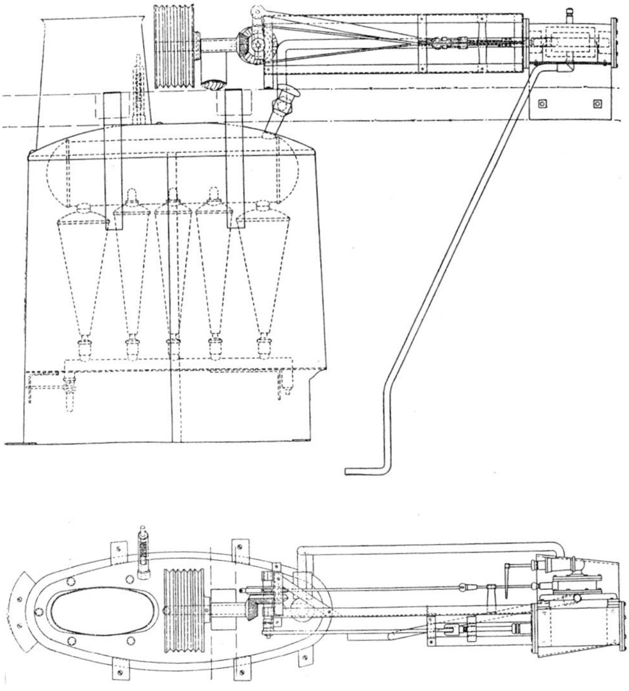

Figure 5. The power plant of the 1848 Stringfellow monoplane.

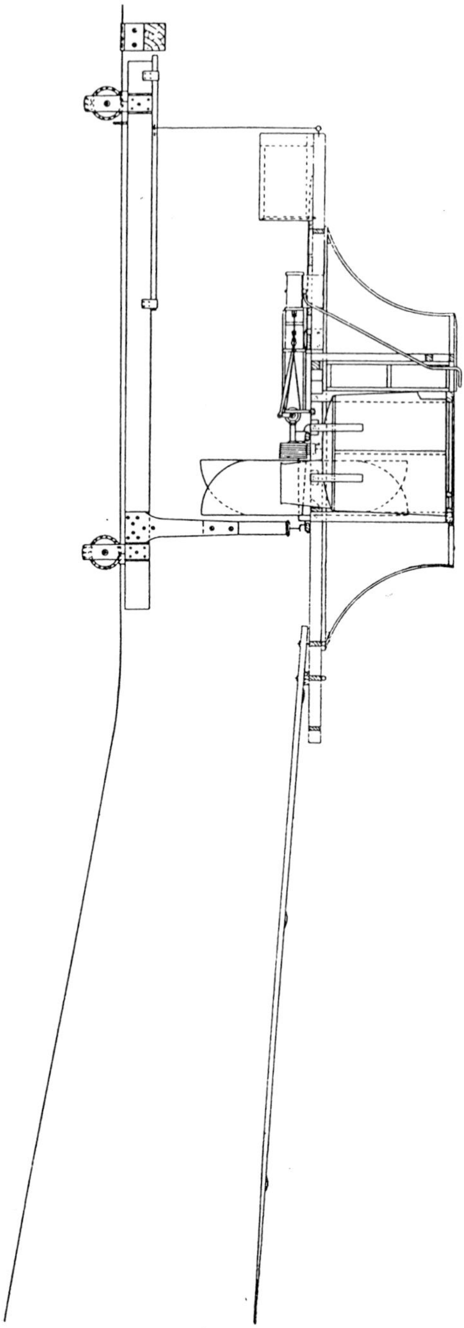

Figure 6. Side elevation of the Stringfellow monoplane on its launching carriage.

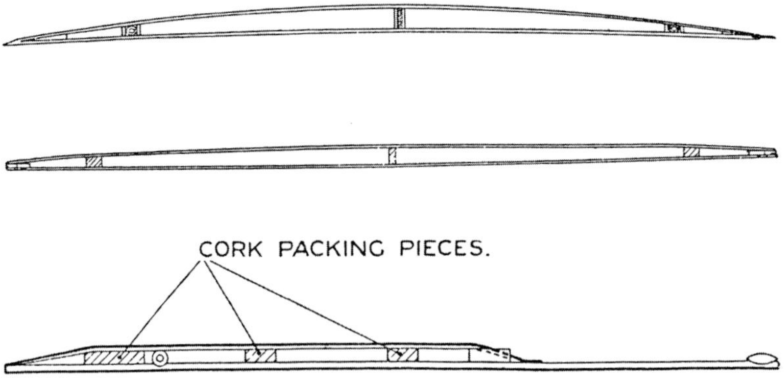

Figure 7. Various wing sections used by Henson and Stringfellow: (top) section proposed by Henson in 1842; (middle) section used in the Henson-Stringfellow model of 1844/47; (bottom) root section of the 1848 Stringfellow monoplane.

Herbert Wenham delivered his classic paper entitled *'Aerial Locomotion'* a monograph written some seven years before it was read. The influence of this paper on Stringfellow was so marked that it caused him to revive his interest in aeronautics.

In the past Sir George Cayley had advocated 'superimposed planes' and his original glider was of a triplane configuration; Wenham's lecture confirmed this to be the way forward. Also at this meeting which was held at the Society of Arts it was proposed to hold an exhibition in 1868. Following this meeting the Honorary Secretary of the Society, F.W. Breary, went to Chard to see Stringfellow and ask for a contribution from the pioneer. Stringfellow had really been waiting for the call and this visit spurred him into action. He confirmed that he would use the idea of superimposed planes and that he would build a model using that format.

The first Aeronautical Exhibition was held in June 1868 at Crystal Palace and Stringfellow contributed three exhibits, as follows:

Class 1 Light Engines & Machinery – No. 4: light engine & machinery for aerial purposes about half horse-power. Cylinder 2 in diameter, 3 in stroke. Generating surface of boiler 3½ ft. Starts 100 lb pressure in three minutes, works two propellers 3 ft in diameter, about 300 rpm, with 3½ pints of water and 18 oz liquid fuel; works about 10 minutes. Weight engine, boiler, water and fuel etc. 16¼ lb.

Class 1 Light Engines & Machinery – No. 5: a one horse-power copper boiler and fireplace, weight about 40 lb, capable of sustaining a pressure of 500 psi.

Class 4 Working Models – No. 37: working model of an aerial steam carriage, the whole, including engine, boiler, water and fuel weighing about 12 lb. Cylinder 1.1875 in diameter, 2 in stroke works two propellers 21 in diameter, about 600 revolutions per minute, steam rises to 100 lb pressure in 5 minutes. On account of steam, the Manager of the Crystal Palace Co. will not allow this or any similar models to show flight in the main building, and it will be necessary, for want of space, to attach it to a line by a travelling pulley. If the distance will allow for the attainment of such speed as the engine is capable of imparting, it will be seen that this model will sustain itself in flight.

Whilst details of engines and other machinery developed by both Henson and Stringfellow are given below it is pertinent to note that the latter was the more important of the two in this department. He built several sets of engines for flying machines during his career and all of them were made with precision and perfection.

The triplane that was exhibited at the Crystal Palace is important, as it was the final aircraft that Stringfellow constructed during his long period of research. He used the format recommended by Wenham and he produced the novel aeroplane that is depicted in fig. 8. It had three rectangular, superimposed planes which decreased in wingspan pro-

Figure 8. The steam triplane built by John Stringfellow.

Figure 9. The engine of the Henson-Stringfellow aeroplane of 1844/47.

gressively downwards; it had fixed horizontal planes both forward and aft of the centre or main plane, with the tailplane merging into the wing. This tail was similar in configuration to that used on the 1848 model. The wings reverted to the type described in the Henson patent specification of 1842 and during the period of development from that time to 1868 several types of section for the ribs were investigated (see fig. 7).

It could be said that this triplane combined all the ideas that were found in its predecessors. The total lifting surface of the wings was stated to be 28 sq. ft whilst the tailplane was more or less identical to that fitted to the 1848 machine; the all-up weight of the triplane, included the power unit, water and fuel was just under 12 lb. This engine, which was more or less identical to the 1844–47 Henson & Stringfellow machine, was said to produce ⅓ hp and could be ready to run within five minutes. The Secretary of the Aeronautical Society, F.W. Breary, commented on this engine at the time, saying 'one-third of the power of a horse, whilst the weight was only that of a goose!'

Since no trial in free flight was allowed in the main hall of the Crystal Palace the model was permitted to run along a wire that was stretched out in a nearby transept for 100 yards, using the launching system previously employed in the 1848 tests. Running down this wire the aircraft was observed to have lifted off and raised the wire 'several feet', and on one occasion, when the wire broke, the machine descended gently down in a glide. These observations were endorsed by the Jurors' Committee of the society. Later, after the Exhibition had closed, the machine was tested further in the basement of the building, where similar results were maintained. Some months afterwards the triplane was 'flown' at Chard, but there a number of minor mishaps occurred, including the burner methylated spirit fuel blowing out, and the wire-based trials were aborted. As a true free flight attempt was never made, for the model was really designed for indoor experiments, the results of all these trials and tests remained inconclusive and one can only conjecture whether the machine was capable of sustained flight.

After the Exhibition, Frederick Breary wrote to Stringfellow on 21 July 1868 to inform him that he had won a prize of £100 Class 1 – Light Engines. The performance of the engine was recorded as follows: Area of piston 3 in, pressure in cylinders 80 psi, length of stroke 3 in, velocity of piston, 150 ft/min., therefore $3 \times 80 \times 150 = 36{,}000$ ft/lb. Visiting engineering enthusiasts were so impressed by the engine that they contributed a further £50 to Stringfellow and with all this money he built a 'long room' at Chard for further experiments. There was, unfortunately, no prize for the triplane.

Engines for Aerial Navigation constructed by Henson and Stringfellow
When discussing the power units constructed by the two pioneers it is necessary to return to the provisions of the 1842 Letters Patent sealed by William Henson, for in that specification may be found the form of engine that instigated the research and how John Stringfellow continued on a similar vein until his last flying machine was built.

It appears that Henson was assisted by an able engineer named John Chapman, who had acted as an adviser upon the enrolment of the 1842 patent and who was well versed in the technology of the steam engines of the time. Chapman also possessed a good knowledge of aerial forces and he was, therefore, the ideal man for the job. At this time there were many critics on the aeronautical scene and they had varying degrees of scientific knowledge – or none at all. The power required to propel a flying machine was a favourite topic of the day and the technical press at the time carried letters ranging from the astute to the plainly ridiculous. Many estimates of power for the 'aerial steam carriage' were made, with one contributor to *Magazine of Science* on 1 April 1843 calculating that 100 hp would be necessary to fly the machine at 50 mph whiles other sages apparently thought that it would need 4,500 hp. John Chapman, writing under the pseudonym 'L.L.' in *Mechanics Magazine*, also on 1 April 1843 tended to support Henson's claims, though in a later edition of the same journal, Sir George Cayley was critical of Henson's monoplane configuration, stating that his triplane theories would be more suited to aerial navigation. Chapman, however, continued to back Henson's plan, saying that of all the schemes then being considered, Henson's was the most likely to succeed.

The outcome of all this publicity convinced Henson after the incorporation of the Aerial Transit Company that he must place the machine properly before the general public and to this end he had a model made which was exhibited at the Adelaide Gallery in the Strand in London; here displays of models worked by clockwork and by steam were given together with lectures which lasted about twenty minutes. The Adelaide model was more or less ready by the end of June 1843. Henson had written to Stringfellow that he had a man named Lodge make an engine for him but it was not satisfactory. Lodge made another and this was, apparently, 'better made'. From items in the press it appears that the first engine virtually shook itself to pieces but the second, which had a single cylinder, had a total weight of only 6 lb and was said to make 1,500 rpm. It seems that the experiments made at the Adelaide Gallery were not successful, for Henson was reported as saying, 'Not a single foot did it fly'.

Presumably these engines were of a similar specification to that described in the patent, which illustrated a twin-cylinder, unidirectional, double-acting unit having overhung cranks and a central flywheel (see fig. 10). The boiler was of a special style which consisted of a series of conical vessels surmounted by a cylindrical drum with the flames of combustion impinging upon the whole of the area of both cones and the underside of the drum. From this design further models, mainly of single-cylinder forms, were produced.

A letter written by Henson to Stringfellow in November 1843 mentioned another engine which had been prepared for the full-sized model, and which he now wished to sell. It referred to a unit with twin cylinders of 7 in bore and 14 in stroke which generated 20 nhp. It was built by Richard Houchin of City Road, London on the recommendation of the celebrated engineer John Farey. What happened to it is unknown, for it seems that this was the only reference to the unit; without doubt it was the first full-sized engine to be made.

The experiments of 1844 and 1847 used a light engine, most certainly built by Stringfellow, consisting of a single-cylinder, double-acting, uni-directional machine with an overhung flywheel all supported by four angle-iron brackets (see Fig. 9). A boiler containing conical vessels and an upper drum, probably with full encasement, was believed to have been provided. This engine had a bore of 1½ in by a stroke of 3 in and could run at 300 rpm.

Stringfellow's 1848 monoplane had an excellent little power unit of a similar type to the 1843 one, but with only two angle rails with a square framework at the opposite end to the cylinder to carry the crankshaft and eccentrics. A drum and cone boiler was used in this case as well.

For the 1868 triplane, Stringfellow again made a single-cylinder steam unit very much in the style of previous efforts, with a drum and cone boiler; the other engine shown in the 1868 exhibition was probably similar in appearance, for it was of near equal size. This latter machine, the prize-winning exhibit, was purchased in February 1887 by the American, Professor Samuel Pierpoint Langley for use in his tandem-wing aircraft experiments; at the same time he also purchased the triplane.

Langley was appointed the Secretary of the Smithsonian Institute in Washington DC in November 1887, and there he continued his investigations into powered flight. As a result of this appointment the Stringfellow engine and triplane were eventually exhibited in the Smithsonian; the latter came there in March 1889. The engine became Inventory No. 1 in the Aeronautical Collection whist the triplane was rebuilt by Melvin Vaniman using some of the original components and replacing others with new ones. The triplane is usually thought to be a replica but this example is much nearer to the original than other models that are exhibited elsewhere.

Apart from the aeronautical steam engines, Stringfellow made a considerable number of small units of small size for industrial use, mainly in lace-making, but one other engine was produced for aeronautical purposes: the twin-cylinder 'French airship' machine, made around 1870. It is known that Stringfellow had contacts in France, having exported his small industrial power units there, and he was

Table 1 *The Henson and Stringfellow steam engines for aeronautical uses.*

	Henson Patent Engine 1843	Stringfellow Engine 1847	Stringfellow Engine 1848	Stringfellow Crystal Palace Engine	Stringfellow Triplane Engine, 1868
Cylinders	2	1	1	1	1
Bore	6 in (approx.)	$1\frac{1}{2}$ in	$\frac{3}{4}$ in	2 in	1.875 in
Stroke	12 in (approx.)	3 in	2 in	3 in	2 in
Bhp	25–30	0.5	0.75	1	–
Rpm	200 (approx.)	254 (approx.)	450 (approx.)	300	600@prop.
Boiler pressure	100 psi	100 psi	100 psi	100 psi	100 psi
Fuel	Alcohol	Alcohol	Alcohol	Alcohol	Alcohol
Weight	600 lb	12 lb	9 lb	$16\frac{1}{4}$ lb	12 lb

Notes: The Prize Award states that the weight of the Crystal Palace Engine was 13 lb. It is worthy of note that only the two Stringfellow engines that were at the 1868 exhibition were shown in steam whose power could be verified. Of the fifteen engines displayed, of which eight were steam, only one other was shown in motion and this was a miniature unit made by Camille Vert.

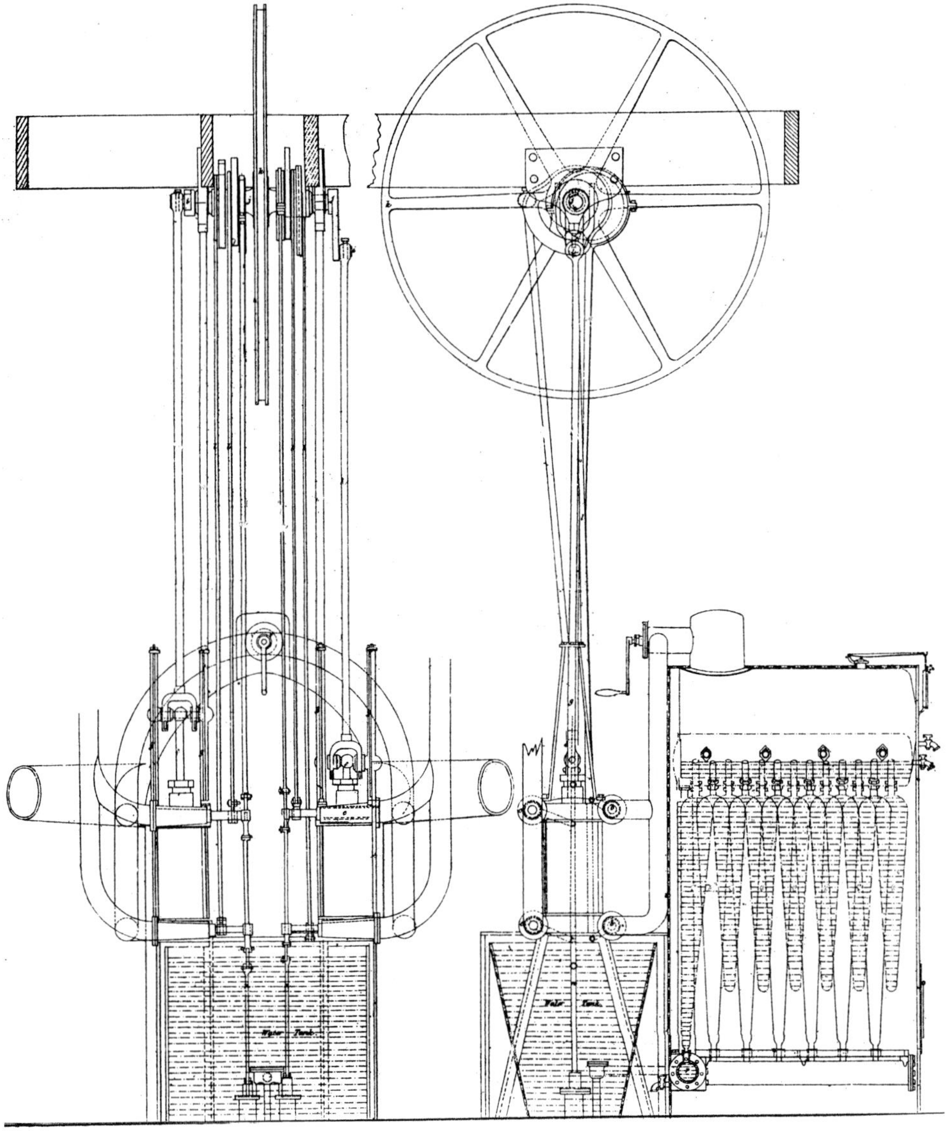

Figure 10. The twin-cylinder steam engine proposed by Henson in his patent specification of 1842.

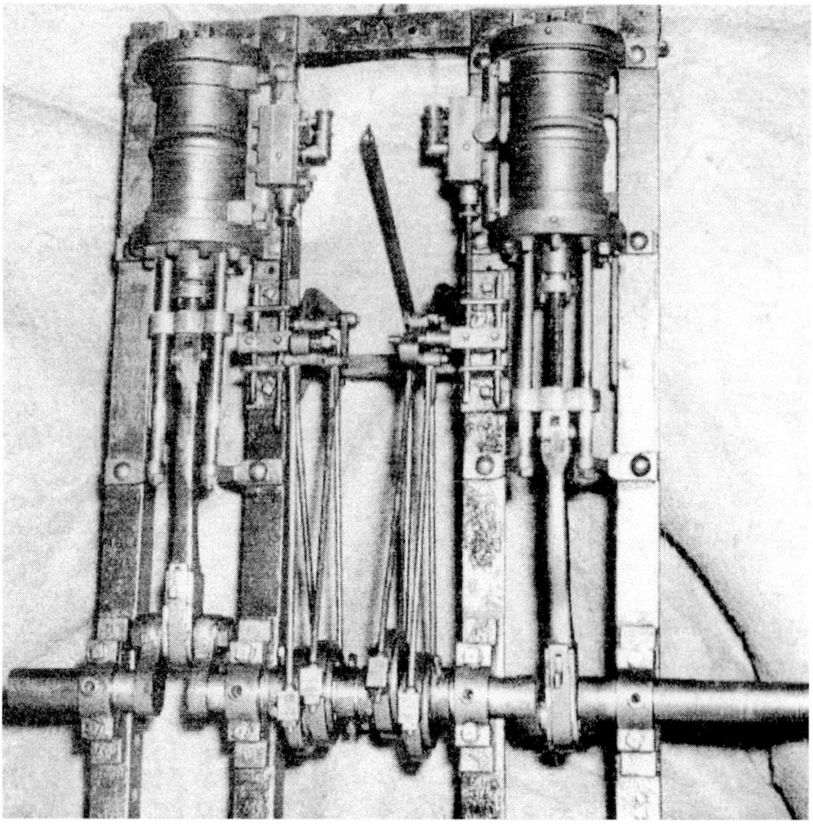

Figure 11. The twin-cylinder engine made by Stringfellow for the 'French airship'. (Courtesy Somerset County Museum).

approached to build a plant to power a small dirigible ordered by the Organization for the Relief of Paris by Balloon. However, the Franco-Prussian War, the reason for the order, was over before the engine was completed and it remained in England. It is still in the Taunton Museum; it is a twin-cylinder, double-acting, reversing unit with cranks set at 90 degrees all mounted upon a strong rectangular iron framework (see fig. 11).

Notes about Boilers used on the Henson and Stringfellow Steam Engines

From documentary evidence it would seem that Henson first proposed the 'drum and cone' type of boiler, for it appeared in the drawings for the 1842 patent specification for 'Locomotive Apparatus for the Air, Land and Water'. This boiler was described as being constructed from copper with screwed joints of brass, and it was stated that by combining a series of conical vessels to a three-drum arrangement a simple unit could be made which provided an extensive heating surface. Although writers have always stated that alcohol fuel was used in the experiments, the patent clearly mentions 'grates and fire-bars' and 'fire and ash-pit doors' which indicates the use of solid fuel.

Stringfellow adopted Henson's 'cone and drum' system but in a simplified form, using only one cylindrical drum. His boilers were all encased and all used alcohol fuel in the form of methylated spirit; they all worked at a pressure of 100 psi and steam could be raised in between three and five minutes from cold (fig. 10 shows drawings of the 1842 pattern of power unit).

It is clear that William Henson and John Stringfellow were the most successful of the early heavier-than-air pioneers who had followed the parameters laid down by Sir George Cayley and who had demonstrated that aerial steam navigation was a real probability instead of an ethereal possibility thought up by dreamers. In the mid-nineteenth century a spate of inventors sought to achieve flight by a number of different methods, including powered balloons, fixed-wing craft, ornithopters and helicopters, and it is worth examining each format individually.

Powered Balloons

There were a number of inventors who toyed with the idea of powered balloons. One or two used steam as a source of power, some used electricity and others adhered to the principle of the 'balloon railway' whereby a power source in the gondola picked up a cable or a chain laid upon the ground to progress along a predetermined path. Whether or not these latter forms of propulsion actually came to fruition is unclear, but what is clear is that the powered balloon was the initial form of controlled aerial transportation.

Henri Jaques Giffard (1825–82)

This French railway engineer is mainly known for his invention of the steam injector to force water into boilers whilst they were under pressure as described in his patent specification of 1858. However, Giffard had a life-long interest in flight, particularly in the field of ballooning, and he is also remembered as being the first person in the history of the world to conduct a sustained, controlled and manned powered flight.

Giffard was employed on the design staff at the works of the Chemin de Fer de. Ste Germaine et Versailles, where he was regarded as an expert on steam generation and boilers. He became interested in ballooning in 1844 when he qualified as a pilot, and thereafter, he assisted Dr Le Berrier in his work on ballooning propulsion using propellers and feathered 'oars' etc. to drive manual airships. This activity was not as fanciful as it may seem; in 2003 a BBC TV team demonstrated that it was possible to build such an aircraft. Carrying on from this work Giffard then went on to draw up specifications for a powered airship in 1851 (Brevet d'Invention No. 12226 of 1851, entitled 'L'Application de Vapeur a la Navigation Aerienne').

Based on the provisions of this 1851 patent specification, Giffard built a full-sized airship the following year and in the evening of 24 September 1852 he took off in his steam-powered dirigible downwind at the Hippodrome in Paris to make a circular, controlled flight, turning to both left and right, of 22 km (14 miles), landing safely at Elancourt. Some details of this pioneering airship make interesting reading. The envelope was 144 ft long and the gas capacity (coal gas or hydrogen) 88,275 cu. ft. The engine was a single cylinder unit having a bore of 4 in and a stroke of 12 in. This drove a propeller which was 12 ft in diameter, which revolved at a rate of 110 rpm, and which was mounted on a shaft

Figure 12. A popular engraving by Perot of Henry Giffard's airship.

which was an extension of the crankshaft. The boiler, which was coal fired, maintained a pressure of 100 psi and the weight of the whole of the power unit was 350 lb. (This weight breakdown was as follows: boiler 250 lb, engine 100 lb.) At a power output of 3 hp the unit gave 117 lb per horse power, and the furnace burnt 150 lb of coal per hour. The overall weight of the airship was 1.5 tons, including fuel and water weighing 560 lb. This included the control car (gondola), which was fitted with a boom and rudder 65 ft in length.

Giffard's 1852 steam airship is shown in a popular engraving of the day by Perot (see fig. 12). A view of a later airship, also from an engraving by Perot, is depicted in fig. 14. In this later dirigible Giffard took off with an assistant named Gabriel Yon at Courcelles in August 1855, but this flight was unsuccessful. This machine was 230 ft long and only 33 ft in diameter, containing 106,000 cu. ft of hydrogen gas. With its longer length to diameter ratio it proved to be unstable in flight; violent pitching developed, and a gasbag became detached inside the net. The craft descended quickly with the envelope split and the gas escaping. The balloonists escaped from the wreckage but the airship

Figure 13. Another representation of Henri Giffard's airship. Note the different styles of envelope.

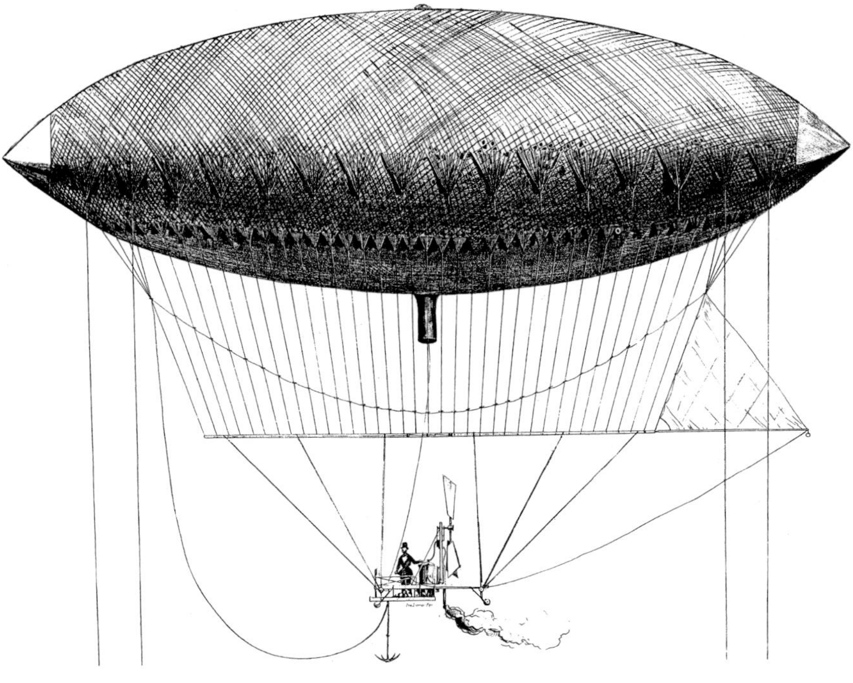

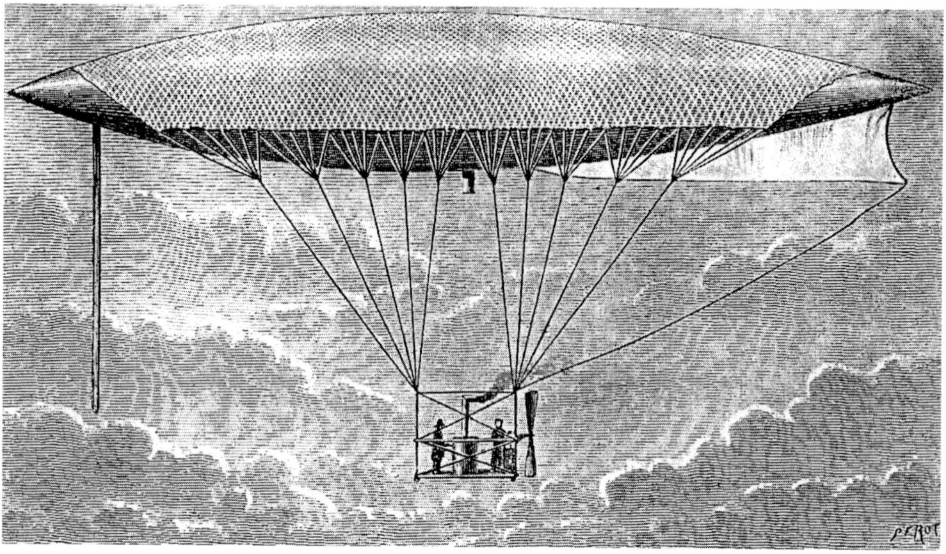

Figure 14. The larger, 1855, version of the Giffard airship, also drawn by Perot.

was completely destroyed when the hydrogen ignited after coming into contact with the boiler.

A further patent was filed along similar lines to the 1851 document and this specified an airship with an 80 hp engine; this was never proceeded with, however, and Giffard continued with balloon experiments where the vehicles were tethered to the ground and allowed to sail aloft using steam winches. He communicated two patents to the UK, concerning this method of controlling captive balloons: Brit. Pat. No. 466 of 1867, entitled 'Balloons' and Brit. Pat. No. 3036, also of 1867 and entitled 'Balloons' but containing improvements on the earlier specification.

Flights with this form of captive balloon were undertaken and at the Paris Exposition of 1867 some were exhibited being controlled by a steam winch as in the patent specifications, to provide rides for the populace. At this exhibition the Empress Eugenie of France graciously received Henri Giffard.

Other large balloons were demonstrated the following year and in 1869 Giffard arrived in London to present a huge aerostat containing 423,500 cu. ft of hydrogen. His final triumph in aerostation occurred in 1878, when he produced an 11 ton balloon with a volume of 882,000 cu. ft to give rides to some 35,000 passengers at the Tuileries.

From 1879 onwards he persevered with work on the dynamics of steam and refrigeration. He committed suicide in 1882.

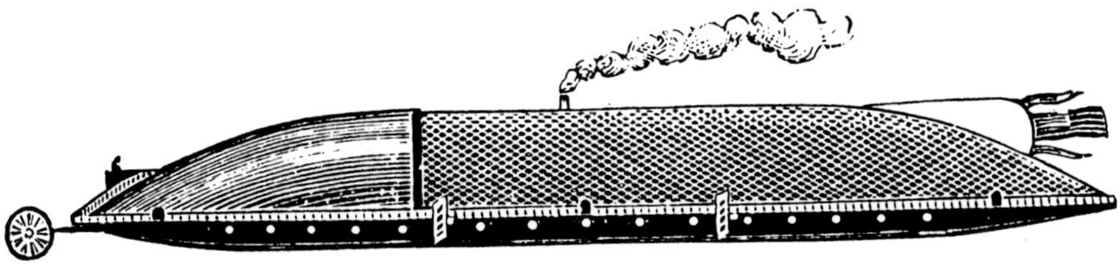

Figure 15. The large steam dirigible proposed by Albert Livingstone Blackman in 1880.

Albert Livingstone Blackman

This inventor produced two patents concerning powered airships which had propelling airscrews and steerage airscrews. His first application, Brit. Pat. No. 985 of 1880, described a rigid envelope with an internal framework but did not specify a power source. However, a later specification sealed the following year described the large steam dirigible shown in fig. 15. Entitled 'Navigable Balloon', it portrayed an elongated envelope which had 'propelling screws' at either side together with a 'steerage screw' which could be located at either or both ends. Machinery for altering the propeller direction was to be provided and a governor was to be fitted for maintaining the ship on an even keel. The rigid framework was retained and it was stated that the chimney was to pass through the whole ensemble of the envelope structure (Brit. Pat. No. 3691 of 1881). A similar scheme was revealed by an Iberian, Julio Cezar Ribeiro de Souza in Brit. Pat. No. 4887 of 1881.

François Folacci

This gentleman communicated a specification which was filed as 'Navigational Balloon' in Brit. Pat. No. 2057 of 1884. The description showed a combination of Giffard's and Blackman's ideas in that it

Figure 16. François Folacci's 'navigable balloon' proposed in 1884.

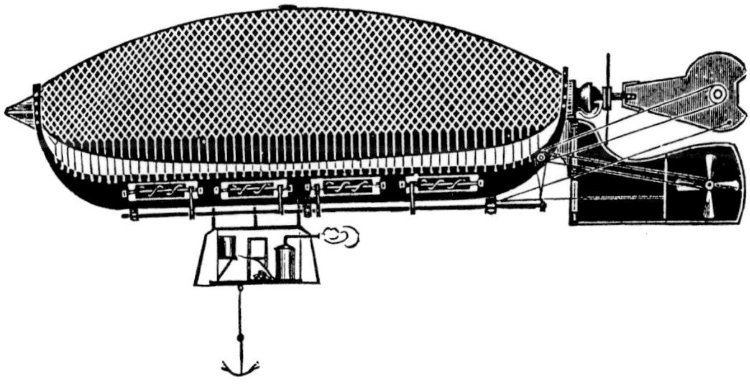

contained a steam engine located in a gondola to drive helical screws within casings along a girder suspended beneath the envelope together with tail fans mounted on universal joints (see fig. 16).

Alphonse Aubrée

Another Frenchman also communicated a specification in 1884 which depicted a bizarre contraption consisting of two pear-shaped balloons at either end of a gondola or 'engine room' containing machinery which actuated oars alongside the casing and a screw propeller at the rear. There was also a rudder. This airship was described in Brit. Pat. No. 15023 of 1884 and is illustrated in fig. 17.

Apart from the above there was a plethora of schemes for 'navigable balloons' that ranged from the impractical to the outright absurd, but it was not until pioneers such as Santos Dumont, Willows and Count Ferdinand von Zeppelin came along, that the airship became a true reality.

Fixed Wing Heavier-than-Air Machines

It was in this area of investigation and invention that success took root. Felix du Temple is credited with building a model able to take off and land safely in the heavier-than-air mode. This paved the way for a number of improvers such as Thomas Moy and Victor Tatin.

Felix du Temple de la Croix (1823–1890)

This Frenchman, more commonly remembered as just Felix du Temple, was a commander in the French navy. He has been given the accolade of having flown the first powered heavier-than-air machine in

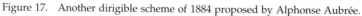

Figure 17. Another dirigible scheme of 1884 proposed by Alphonse Aubrée.

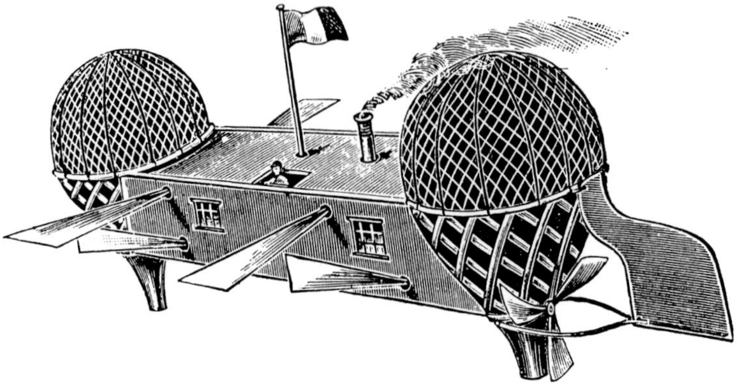

history. Research by Captain J.L. Pritchard in collaboration with A.M. Ballantyne appears to show that the Stringfellow experiments were not as successful in maintaining sustained flight as was previously supposed and that the real originator was, indeed, Felix du Temple in 1857.

Du Temple commenced his studies in aeronautics during the early 1850s and he arrived finally at an erudite design in 1857; he filed a patent specification in that year (Brevet d'Invention No. 32031 of 1857, 'Locomotive Aérienne par Imitation du Vol des Oiseaux'). This specification described a boat style fuselage with cross-braced triangular wings attached to it and a generous triangulated tailplane. It had a wingspan of 56 ft and any suitable power plant ranging from steam or hot-air engines to the newly invented Lenoir internal combustion engine; a fan-like propeller having twelve blades was envisaged. Using this patent specification as a basis du Temple went on to produce a small model weighing about 1½ lb, which was originally powered by clockwork and then by steam. This ingenious model was demonstrated and it was found that it was able to take off, sustain itself in the air and land safely. It was thus the first craft to achieve three of the four main parameters of powered flight; it lacked only the fourth, being 'controlled', for it controlled itself when in free flight. Drawings of this model are shown in fig. 18 and colour section page 4.

After this success with the model aircraft the Frenchman decided to build a full-sized version. It was similar in aspect to the model, and it possessed all of the attributes of a modern aeroplane, with a tractor airscrew, a power plant amidships, a tailplane and rudder. The airscrew was said to have been a twelve-bladed unit of 13 ft in diameter. Steam was used as the method of propulsion and was raised in the du Temple style of torpedo-boat boiler.

There is conflicting evidence concerning the constructional details of the full-sized aircraft. Although it had been established that it was a monoplane with forward set wings of 40 ft span, and although, as the writer has said said, some authorities have suggested that the propeller had twelve blades, others have said that it had six; to add to the confusion another illustration possibly shows eight! Again there are claims that the undercart was retracting, but the same illustration seems to depict a fixed unit. In the ninth *Report of the Aeronautical Society of Great Britain* it is stated that the power unit may have been motivated by hot air, for it says:

> *The motive power is a hot-air engine with two cylinders 18 in in diameter being constructed of thin steel strengthened by rings of the same material,*

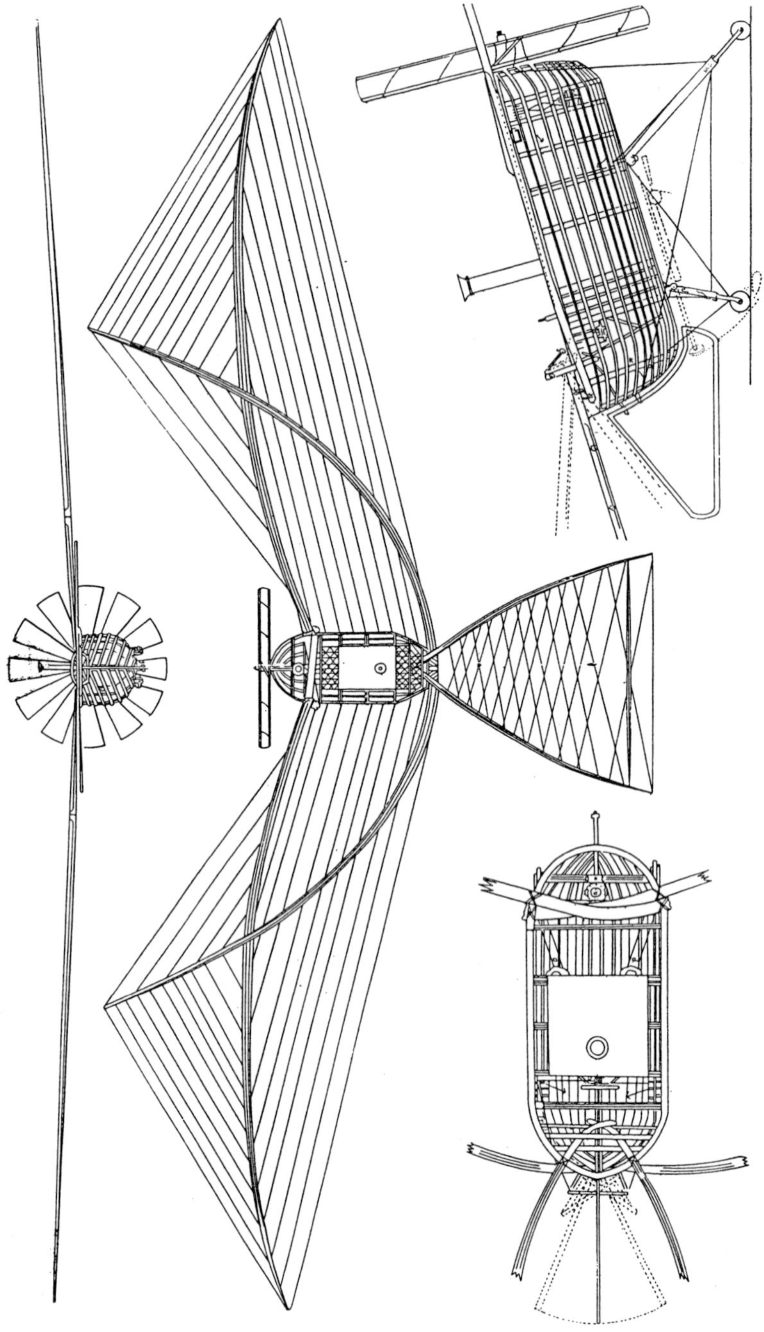

Figure 18. Line drawings of the monoplane devised by Felix du Temple.

the cylinders carry the piston guides and also safety valves, the bottoms of the cylinders are exposed to the fire, the fuel being petroleum. The machine is propelled by a 13 ft, six-bladed screw.

The total weight of the power source was 160 lb. The writer believes that there were probably two distinct engines, the hot-air version noted in the report and a steam alternative using the same cylinders but connected to a du Temple style of boiler.

Charles Dollfus, in his *'Histoire de l'Aeronautique'*, published in 1932 says that a flight attempt was made at Brest in 1874 using this machine. Apparently, tethered tests were made at first, but later on it was believed that it was launched down a ramp to become airborne for a short, faltering 'hop' before being pulled to the ground by gravity and rolling over on its side. Some versions of the story recount that a 'young sailor' acted as the pilot on this occasion, but others suggest that du Temple himself was at the controls. Whatever the identity of the aeronaut, this 'flight' was neither sustained nor controlled, and it has not been recorded whether steam or hot air was the propulsive method. However, the failure of this experiment, in no way negates du Temple's claim to fame.

Nikolai Teleshov

One of the first aeronautical designs to be documented in Russia was for a fantastic 120-passenger, steam-driven, 'flying wing' airliner in 1864 (fig. 19). This extraordinary device was patented in Great Britain under the title of 'Flying Machines' (Brit. Pat. No. 2299 of 1864), and it was jointly communicated by Teleshov and Gustave de Struve (who may have been the patent agent in Russia). The preamble to the specification states that the aircraft was projected to carry 120 persons at a rate of 30 mph. It would have a large concave 'aeroplane' surface around the body or fuselage for floating on air and a propeller driven by a vee-twin steam engine with cranks set at 90 degrees was fitted at the rear of the body, while both vertical and horizontal 'rudders' were provided for lift and steerage. A weighted regulator was incorporated to maintain the centre of gravity as near as possible, and the machine was specified to be started down a ramp in order to gain velocity before ascending into the air. Its vast scale can be seen in the drawing. The central engine room with a two-cylinder power unit (which may have been of the oscillating variety), located above the boiler room with its twin steam generators, the railed-in promenade deck surrounding the 'wheelhouse', and the long fuselage containing the passenger accommodation, all contributed to its immense size. The only item that

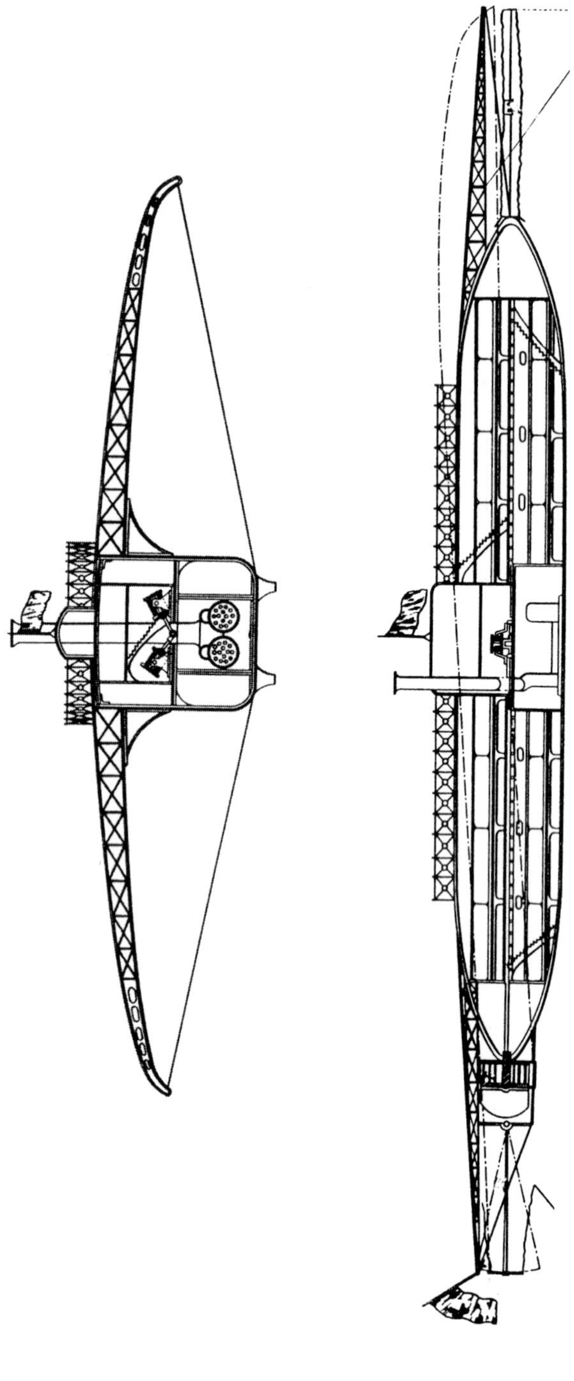

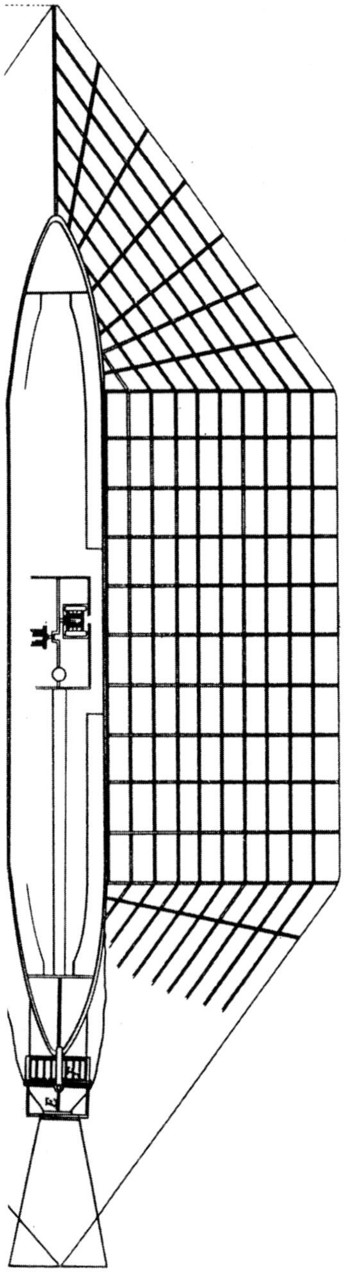

Figure 19. The 'Flying Wing' airliner proposed by the Russian inventor Nikolai Teleshov in 1864.

it lacked as a 'ship of the sky' was the anchor so beloved of the balloonists. One would have thought that this creation was a product of the nautical mind, but this was not the case, for Teleshov was an artillery officer in the Russian army.

One may speculate about the materials to be used in the construction of this behemoth; the wing with its X-braced struts and longerons would have had to been made from aluminium or one of its alloys and the engine must have been a very lightweight unit. Needless to say, this aeroplane was never built, but the inventor's mind did have a modern quirk, for the machine does look similar to today's representations of alien spaceships.

Having described the monster airliner, Teleshov went on to patent another machine which was remarkably modern. This was a delta-wing craft, very reminiscent of the Concorde layout in plan view, which was designed to be driven by a 'reaction-motor' – in other words jet propelled. Other novel features of this machine, for its time, were the use of the geodetic form of construction for the fuselage and the triangulated bracing system used in the wing formation. Steam or compressed air could have been the power source for this project, which, like Teleshov's other design, was never made. The specification for the delta-wing craft was patented in France under the title of 'Wings' and it is to be found in Brevet d'Invention No. 77550 of 1867. There is no doubt in the writer's mind that, using modern technology, this aircraft would have flown, and it shows great foresight on the part of the inventor (see fig. 20).

Figure 20. The delta-wing craft designed by Nikolai Teleshov in 1867.

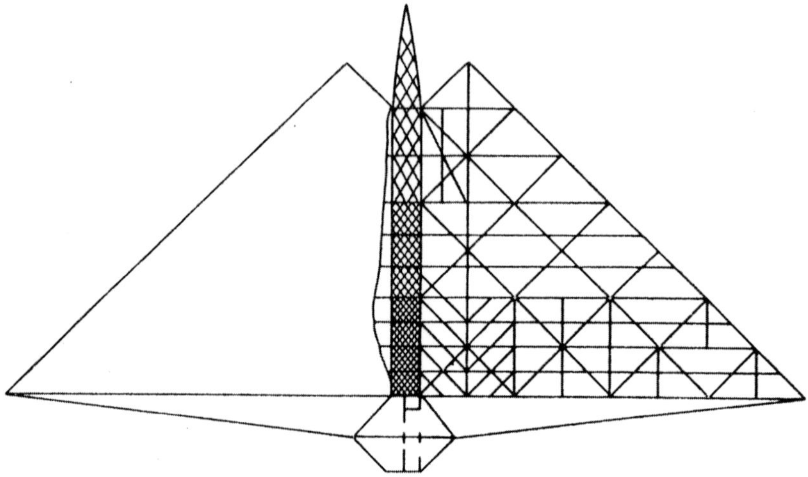

James Butler and Edmund Edwards

The aircraft that was projected by James Butler and Edmund Edwards was also propelled by reaction; it was described in Brit. Pat. No. 2115 of 1867. Again, it was of delta-wing formation and resembled a paper dart (see fig. 21).

It was simple in construction, consisting of two triangular planes set on top of a vertical member, called the web in the specification. This web housed the steam generator and a pipe led from it and terminated in a nozzle at the rear, where the steam under pressure was discharged with force to drive the machine forward by reaction. Curiously, the inventors stated, 'When steam power is employed, the aeroplane may be made hollow for condensing the steam, and thus save weight by using the same water repeatedly'. This sounds absurd, for if the steam was used for reactive propulsion it would have condensed to atmosphere, with the water so generated falling to the earth! However, their other statement in the specification made more sense, for they said that if the machine rested on a carriage with wheels, then when the speed on the ground became sufficient, the air beneath the planes would allow the craft to rise. If a model based upon these principles were made and launched by hand, the project would definitely have worked. The patent specification also suggested that compressed air or inflammable gas could be used as alternative power sources.

At this time in the mid-nineteenth century other inventors came up with the idea of jet propulsion. Richard Boyman and James Nelson both advocated 'jets of fluid' escaping from reservoirs or generators in 1867.

Thomas Moy

Thomas Moy was an independent experimenter who built a large flying machine which rejoiced in the name of the 'Aerial Steamer' in 1874 (see fig. 22). The aircraft was tested a year later at the Crystal Palace, where it provided some interesting data.

Figure 21. The paper-dart style of aeroplane that was invented by Butler and Edwards.

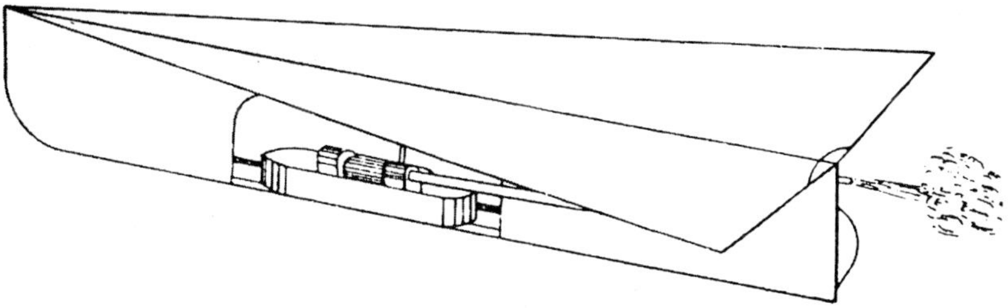

Figure 22. A photograph of the period showing the construction of Thomas Moy's 'aerial steamer', as tested at the Crystal Palace.

Moy was a patent agent by profession, and he was a member of the Aeronautical Society of Great Britain and therefore one of that band of aeronautical experimenters that abounded during the nineteenth century. These pioneers fell into two groups: 'groundsmen' and 'airmen'. The former tended to get bogged down in scientific research and to 'fly' aircraft that were really 'test-rigs', whilst the latter did attempt to get aloft to make proper flights, despite the danger to themselves; Moy was a 'groundsman'.

In 1874 he filed a patent specification for a peculiar, large, steam-driven, tandem-wing monoplane. In collaboration with R.E. Shill, who had made a steam 'turbine injector' power unit which was shown at the 1868 Crystal Palace Exhibition, he constructed a full-sized version of the patent prototype and tested it on a circular track at the Crystal Palace in 1875. The machine was never intended to go into free flight but was designed only to lift up and remain airborne in a 'round-the-pole' experiment. To do this the Great Fountain at the Crystal Palace was boarded over to form a continuous track 300 ft in diameter upon which the 'steamer' was to run. A rope fixed to the centre of the fountain enabled the machine to describe continuous circles around it.

The layout of the 'aerial steamer' was similar to that used by Professor Samuel Langley some twenty years later, and it was probably based upon the work done by D.S. Brown, a member of the ASGB who had tested the stability of a series of tandem-wing models in 1873 and 1874 (Brit. Pat. No. 411 of 1872). The ninth annual report of the ASGB included some interesting details concerning the characteristics of the Moy aeroplane. The steam engine, which was of Moy's own design, produced 3 hp and weighed 80 lb; it had a single, double-acting cylinder having a bore of 2.125 in with a stroke of 3 in. The tubular boiler worked at a pressure of 160 psi and had 8 sq. ft of heating surface to be fired with methylated spirit. This power unit was encased within a housing, which measured 27 in × 27½ in ×7½ in, installed between the two planes. The maximum rpm of the engine was stated to be 800, but the general operating speed was given as 536 rpm, which in turn drove the two propellers or 'wing-planes' as Moy called them, at 67 rpm. The performance of this engine was quite satisfactory, for with the safety valves set to blow off at 140 psi, and with the engine cut-off at ½ stroke, it gave a value of 99.696 ft/lb per minute to produce 3.02 hp. The airscrews could have their pitch altered; when set at 15 degrees to the vertical the pressure was exactly 1 lb per sq. ft, whilst if set at an angle of 45 degrees a pressure of 1½ lb per sq. ft could be achieved. It was estimated that with 15 degrees of incidence a thrust of 56½ lb could be maintained, and with 45 degrees some 84.8 lb.

In the airframe, the plane in front of the engine was 50 sq. ft in area whilst that behind was 65 sq. ft; the front plane had an incidence of 10 degrees in order to gain lift. The total weight of the craft was 214 lb which was about 1¼ lb per sq. ft of wing area, and it was calculated that a speed of 35 mph around the track would be sufficient to enable lift to be achieved. However, in the tests of June 1875 the maximum speed attained around the circular track was only 12 mph, and this was just enough to enable the 'aerial steamer' to lift off between 2 and 6 in from the ground, the first time a full-sized, steam-driven, heavier-than-air machine had achieved 'lift-off'.

Thomas Moy himself had this to say about the proceedings on that day: 'With plenty of steam to spare, it formed a pretty sight in the bright sunshine', but '... the transverse stability was better than the longitudinal stability, but both were bad!' The ninth ASGB report also said:

> *Notwithstanding the fact that the three small carriage wheels were disproportionate to the size of the machine, and that they were made to go*

straight forward, and not to turn in a circle, if self-propulsion ... was capable of being tried upon a much smaller scale, in neglect of which some hundreds of pounds were being expended unnecessarily.

In other words a small model to test the theory would have been better. Nevertheless, Moy did achieve his place in history inasmuch as his craft became airborne of its own volition. His work, however, did not add very much to the knowledge of the day. It is interesting to observe that the two pictures depicting the 'wing-planes' (see figs 22 and 23) showed different versions, one with laminated planking and the other with a smooth face and rounded edges. Both, however, show the method of altering their incidence to provide differing thrust values.

Thomas Moy was responsible for filing three patents concerning aeronautics in the 1870s: the base patent in collaboration with Richard Shill (Brit. Pat. No. 3238 of 1871); improvements to this Brit. Pat. No. 2808 of 1874, and a specification describing steam power units entitled 'Boilers and Engines' (Brit. Pat. No. 1406 of 1877). In 1891 he also filed a patent for 'Governing Aerial Machines' by a pendulum apparatus (Brit. Pat. No. 14742 of that year).

After the Crystal Palace tests Moy planned to construct a much larger machine built along the same lines, which would have had a

Figure 23. A slightly different version of Thomas Moy's 'aerial steamer'. Note the different propellers.

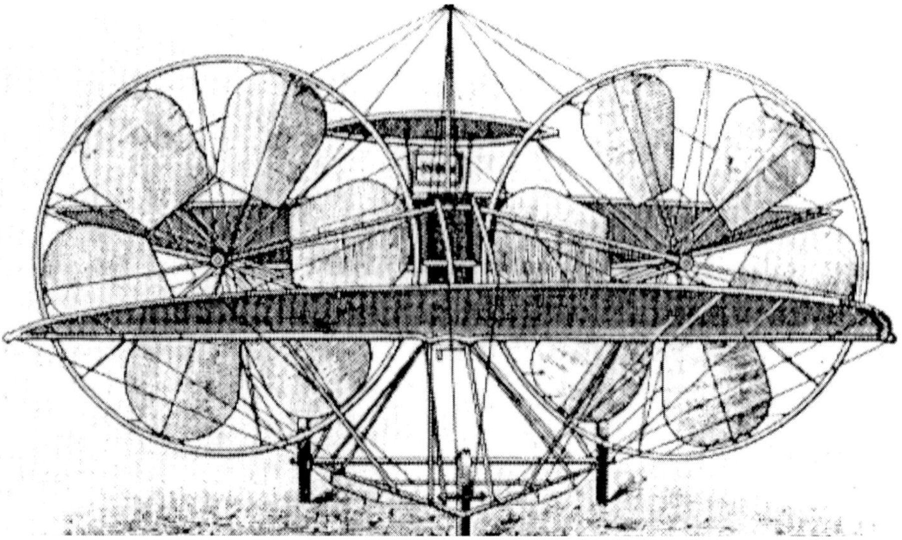

power unit having an output of 100 hp and be able to carry several men in order to '... secure intelligent control while in action'. Alas, he did not have the finance to fund any further schemes, and, in 1879, after investigating the properties of propellers and wing sections etc. he made a small, tandem-wing model with two tractor propellers operated by twisted rubber, which he called a 'military kite'. It never flew.

Victor Tatin (1843–1913)

Tatin was another Frenchman, who experimented with heavier-than-air ornithopters and fixed-wing aircraft, and who had a certain amount of success at the end of the 1870s. He conducted some tests using rubber-powered ornithopters, but apparently abandoned this style of propulsion in favour of the fixed wing and powered tractor propellers. He built a large model aeroplane which was operated by compressed air and was the precursor of a larger steam-propelled machine which was made in the late 1890s in collaboration with Charles Richet (see chapter 3). The compressed-air model was remarkably modern in appearance as may be seen from the illustration in figs 24 and 25. This machine had a wingspan of 6 ft 3½ in, and in plan view it had the traditional location of wings, fuselage and tail surface; however, it lacked any vertical or steerage surface, presumably because it was only used in a tethered 'round-the-pole' mode.

The machinery was contained inside a nacelle type of bodywork to which were attached separate port and starboard

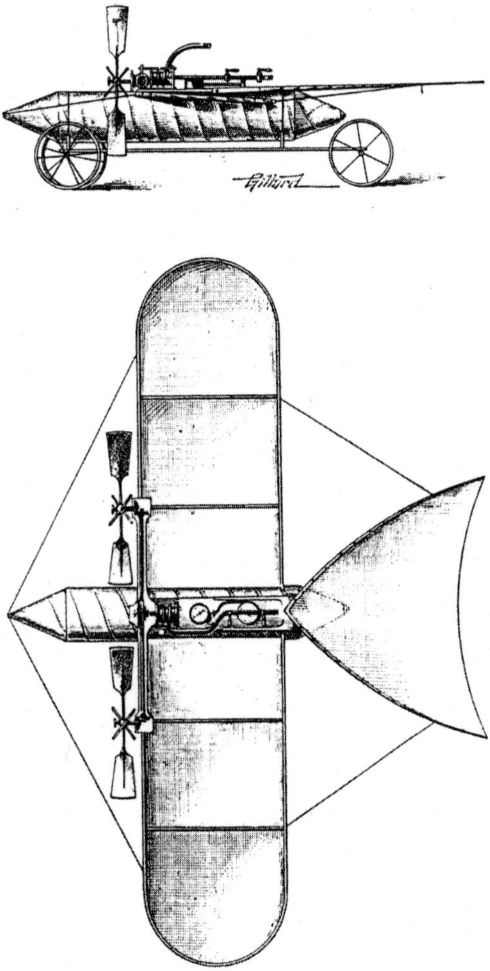

Figure 24. Victor Tatin's model of 1879.

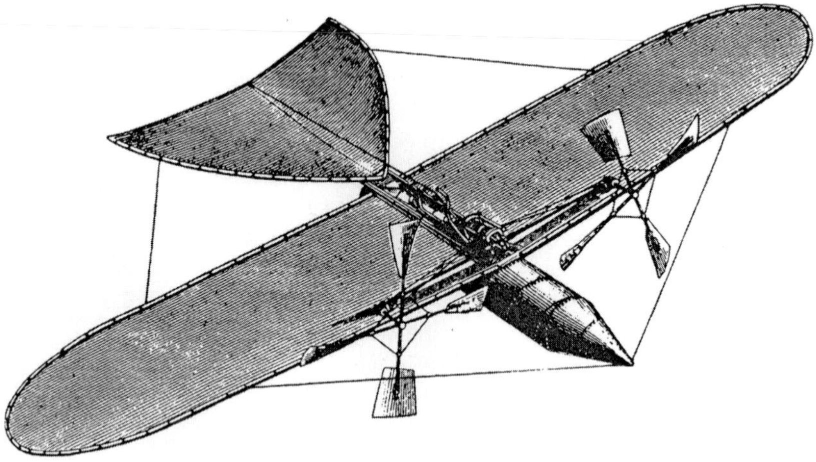

Figure 25. The 1879 Tatin monoplane shown in an attitude of flight.

wings and the tailplane, all braced together with wires. The power unit was simplicity itself, for it consisted of a reservoir containing air under pressure surmounted by a small dome, which had a common pipe for charging and the admission of air to the engine. In the picture, the aft valve allows charging to take place when the admission valve is shut and vice versa. The single cylinder was set in a framework atop the air receiver and this drove a cross shaft which had bevel wheels at its extremities, with the shafting and the gearing enclosed in a tubular casing. These bevel wheels, in turn, drove individual propeller shafts into each screw.

Tatin flew his creation in the 'round-the-pole' mode in 1879, and using an upward incidence of between 8 and 10 degrees to the horizontal on the main plane achieved a 'flight' of nearly 50 ft. The illustration taken from a popular representation by Gillard clearly shows the layout of the model.

Ornithopters (Heavier-than-air flapping-wing craft)

The earliest ideas on powered flight were centred around imitating the way that birds flew. Leonardo da Vinci laid the foundations of ornithopter technology in the fifteenth century, and he demonstrated through tests and drawings the relationship between bird flight and the mechanical flying machine; however, although his theories were scientifically correct, da Vinci never made such a machine. Aeronauts from time immemorial attempted to fly using wings strapped to their bodies and they all suffered injury or even death. It was not until the ninteenth century that the mechanical ornithopter was born. However, whilst the idea was viable in very small models, it was not at all satisfactory in larger sizes or in full-sized aircraft.

John Kinnersley Smythies

In 1860 Smythies filed a patent in the UK which described a flapping-wing aircraft with a special tubular boiler which presented a large heating area combined with a condensing system, all of which was

Figure 26. The method of steam propulsion advocated by John Smythies for his ornithopter, which was described in 1867.

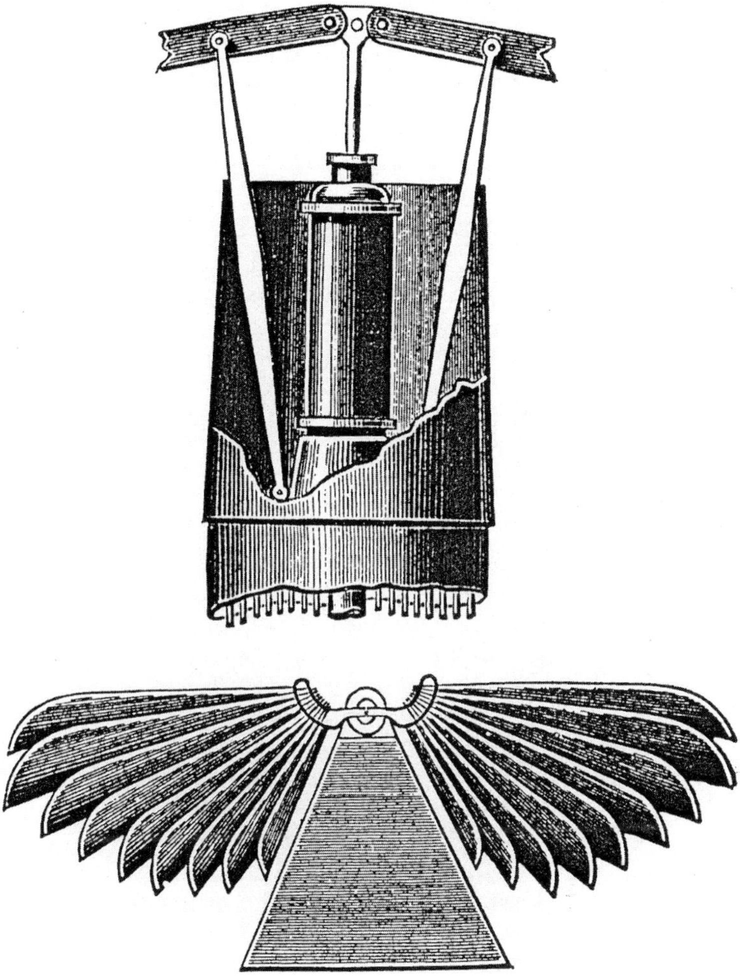

very light. The condenser consisted of a hollow plane made from steel rods covered with oiled silk; the condensed water ran to its lowest part to be pumped back into the steam generator. This patent (Brit. Pat. No. 561 of 1860) did not discuss the form of steam engine to be employed but it hinted at flapping wings made from feathers stiffened by rods, presumably on their leading edges. These wings worked in a compound manner, with the rods overlapping the flexible edge to allow the feathers to beat downwards to provide lift and an extra feather on the end set at an angle to provide propulsion. Apparently the 'rider' steered the machine like a motorcyclist by leaning into a bend whilst 'elastic legs' allowed the machine to land safely!

In 1867 Smythies demonstrated his method of powering the ornithopter, which is shown in the line drawing in fig. 26. His British Patent No. 2504 of that year, entitled 'Steam Flying Machine' depicted a vertically mounted steam cylinder which actuated a pair of feathered flapping wings. The other details in the patent specification were concerned with the boiler etc. found in the earliest one. In this case the tail acted as the condenser. All of this information was repeated in a further specification (Brit. Pat. No. 4151 of 1875), and by 1882 a version of the whole machine was published, together with all the previous matter. These ideas surfaced again in Brit. Pat. No. 7 of 1884; the only new information was that the flapping wings were 'feathered' on the up stroke, possibly by an angle of 30–40 degrees to increase their efficiency.

The final version of this ornithopter is shown in fig. 27, but is not recorded whether he ever made it.

Figure 27. The final form of John Smythies' ornithopter, which was described as 'flapping wings mounted on a steam carriage'.

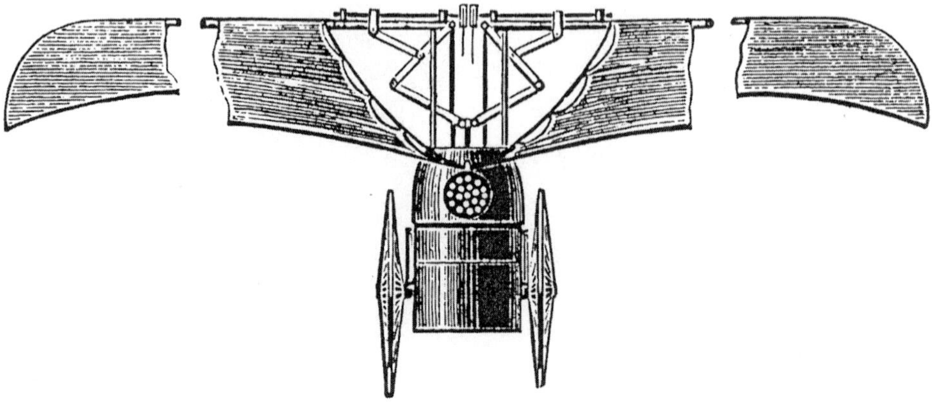

Marc Séguin
This well-known French inventor, who was the nephew of the famous aeronaut, Joseph Montgolfier, was credited with the construction of the first steam locomotive to run on rails in France, but he was also interested in the science of flight. In 1864 he designed a steam-driven ornithopter which is illustrated in fig. 28, a line drawing taken from a sketch made by his son on 26 January 1864. This aircraft had a four-cylinder double-acting steam engine which had cranks set at 180 degrees and the flapping mechanism driven off rods attached to the engine crossheads.

Figure 28. The steam-driven ornithopter proposed by Marc Séguin in 1864.

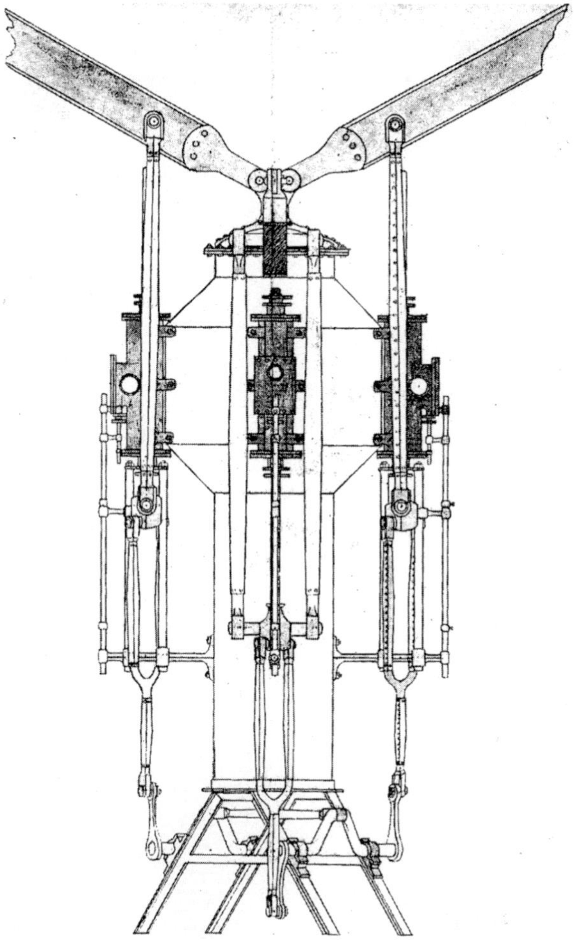

Joseph Meyers Kaufmann

This Glaswegian patented a steam ornithopter in 1867 and in that year he actually built a model of it and demonstrated it at the first Aeronautical Exhibition at Crystal Palace in June 1868. A representation of this machine, taken from an indistinct portion of an engraving depicting the scene at the Exhibition, is illustrated in fig. 29.

In the text of the specification (Brit. Pat. No. 473 of 1867) Kaufmann indicated the method of actuation of the flappers and how the machine was constructed. He stated that there was a 'car' or fuselage which contained the power unit and which was mounted upon wheels to allow it to run forward before taking off; it was also stated that this car could float to enable it to rise off water. The steam engine which powered the wings was connected to them by 'pillow-blocks' which caused an oscillating motion to ensure that they struck the air at angles both in the up and down strokes to create a 'wedging or screwing' motion through the air.

The configuration was of a composite form, comprising both flapping and fixed wings. The flapping wings were set on top of the 'car' in the way described but there were also four narrow fixed wings superimposed one over the other, probably to provide permanent lift as the flappers propelled the craft along. Another curious feature of this craft was the provision of 'buffers' which, when forced out by steam pressure, shot the vehicle into the air at the precise moment of flight. It seems that the machine was designed to fly in the following way: steam was raised and the engine started to flap the wings; this enabled the ensemble to run along the ground on its wheels and when sufficient velocity had been achieved the main planes provided lift enough for the flappers to propel it in flight. Unfortunately the reality was somewhat different for at the Aeronautical Exhibition,

Figure 29. The ornithopter that was exhibited at the Aeronautical Exhibition of June 1868 at the Crystal Palace.

Kaufmann's ornithopter was tried out using a stationary boiler and a flexible pipe. The machine flapped its wings vigorously, leaping up and down until the whole thing disintegrated in a cloud of steam.

Kaufmann's proposed full-sized ornithopter was to have had the following weights and dimensions: 40 hp steam engine weighing 2½ tons designed to flap wings at 120 strokes per minute; each wing to be 35 ft in length and (possibly) 6 ft chord; wing area, a possible 420 sq. ft. It will be seen from this brief description that the design was totally impractical; the stated wing area would certainly not have supported the power unit, let alone the airframe as well. The method of propulsion was equally fatuous for the flapping wings would have had a tip speed 200 ft per second, which would have to be attained in each forward and backward stroke three times a second! Even with today's materials and technology this would be a very tall order – in 1869 it was pure fantasy. It was no wonder, therefore, that his 40 lb model blew up at the first attempt.

The inventors of the nineteenth century often had fanciful ideas when offering their wares, and Kaufmann was no exception. He said that in addition to the ornithopter a tender could be towed behind it to carry fuel, water and stores and behind that cars could be conveyed, all of them possessing suitable 'aeroplanes' to ensure that they would lift off in turn and stay aloft when the whole equipage took flight – an 'aerial steam train' in effect!

Kaufmann also filed a provisional patent concerning various bits of apparatus connected with boiler safety on his machine. He described a special safety valve which warned the 'attendant' if steam pressure was too high. This consisted of pistons and a mercury gauge working in conjunction with a whistle. Another part of the same specification described oil flow to the furnace to control steam pressure and mass (Brit. Pat. No. 1525 of 1867).

Edward Purkis Frost (1842–1922)

Edward Frost was a country squire and therefore had the means and the time to pursue his scientific interests. He lived at West Wratting Hall in Cambridgeshire and was Deputy Lieutenant of the county as well as being a Justice of the Peace. He was one of those gifted amateurs that abounded in the nineteenth century and, like Cayley before him, he did much to expand the vistas of science and technology at that time. He did much to advance the cause of flying, and as well as building two full-sized aircraft of his own, he became a founder member of the Royal Aero Club and a Vice-President and President (from 1908 to 1911), of the Royal Aeronautical Society. He was also a member of the Council of the Aerial League of Great Britain and Ireland. Among his friends were a number of influential people of the time, many of whom involved themselves with his work or took an interest in it, including King Edward VII, Lord Rendlesham, Sir James Douglas, Lord Baden-Powell and the Wright brothers.

He was a remarkable man and seemed to live life to the full; apart from his aeronautical pastimes, he was one of the foremost livestock breeders in the kingdom, with the oldest flock of Suffolk sheep at the time, dating from 1810, and he was a prominent exponent of the Shire horse. He also had a military bent, he joined the Cambridgeshire Mounted Rifles (Volunteers) in 1861 and he even offered himself for active service in 1915 at the age of 73!

Frost commenced his study of flight in 1868, using the assumption that wings in nature are merely beaten up and down and that it was the flexibility and the peculiarity of wing form that enable a bird or a flying mammal to adopt different angles and positions during a particular wing beat; of course this assumption was incorrect as bird flight is a complex exercise controlled by a combination of wing section, wing configuration and changes to them, together with 'fine-tuned' muscular actions in order to take advantage of all conditions of airflow. Robert Burton in his book *Bird Flight* outlined this complexity, as indeed, did Leonardo da Vinci several centuries earlier, and modern research has enhanced our knowledge of the mechanics of birds flight. However, Frost did have half the story; having observed dead pheasants still gliding earthward in a seemingly controlled manner after being shot, he knew that an aerofoil section and wing area had a lot to do with sustained flight.

From this starting point he attempted to reproduce a bird's wing using a system of artificial feathers attached to a framework of wood. His 'feathers' were made from a quill constructed of red willow strengthened with cane let into shallow grooves in the wood and bound with twine; each feather was some 14 ft long, but they only weighed 16 oz. His wings were also made from a framework of red willow, which was covered in silk to which the feathers were attached; over eighty feathers were fixed to each wing. Like Smythies before him Frost made his wings with a rigid anterior edge and a flexible or yielding posterior edge. Their action was stated to be as follows: as the wing beat downwards the flexible tips of the feathers came into play, being made to spread outwards, upwards and forwards in order to create a combination of required lift and drive. The dimensions were: wing span about 35 ft; body length 20 ft; body width 9 ft.

Having made a suitable wing which appeared to have the characteristics of lift, Frost went on to construct a flying machine in which to test his theories and to enable him to achieve powered flight. Construction commenced in 1870, but was not complete until 1877. It was built at West Wratting Hall and Frost had the assistance of the estate carpenter and a Mr Howes from Cambridge. The resulting machine (see page 5 in the colour section) was a strange creation. It had a rigid base mounted upon four wheels, which carried the steam machinery, the framework for the main planes and the power mechanism. The airframe consisted of a foreplane to which two aerofoil wings were attached to the port and starboard sides; behind this there were the two sets of 'power wings', one above the other, and beyond this on the centre line of the craft there was a rudimentary 'tail' which did not have a vertical surface to act as a rudder. The way in which the aircraft was to be controlled was as follows. The machinery flapped the 'power wings' up and down with the flexibility the writer has mentioned to create the required lift, whilst the pilot actuated the foreplane and the fixed wings to provide steerage and auxiliary lift. To fly the machine the engine was connected to the rear wheels by chain drive and the whole ensemble was run up to about 20 mph with the flapping mechanism working simultaneously. After a short run it should have leapt into the air. It was not to be, for the 5 hp steam engine fitted was underpowered for the job and the ornithopter did not even get off the ground. In 1891, Sir James Douglas gave the opinion that if a lightweight internal combustion engine of about 30 hp could have been procured the machine would have probably flown in some way.

The method of construction and of operation showed that Frost had a good grasp of mechanics, for his machine had complex mechanisms which had to work with some degree of co-ordination. The 'power wings' were driven by a combination of rocking beams and levers from the steam engine which was mounted on the platform below; there were two pairs of these wings, upper and lower, and they were driven from different parts of the engine. The top pair were connected to side attachments on the drive mechanism whilst the bottom pair had rocking beams connected to an eyebolt at the top of the engine. From the 2 ft stroke developed at the engine this was increased to 4 or 5 ft at the wing extremity; the upper wings were fitted with kingposts and bracing wires and there was a direct attachment to their lower counterparts so that each pair flapped in unison. A fulcrum point along the centre line of the craft allowed the wings to flap in a controlled manner. As the writer has stated, all of this apparatus was mounted on a four-wheeled carriage with unequal-sized wire wheels fore and aft, which supported a composite arrangement of tubes, rods and a flat platform on which the power unit was fitted and where the pilot control station was situated. In fig. 30 Mr Frost is shown standing at the 'power wing' fulcrum point adjusting the rigging which connected the two top planes. It is strange that he did not make the carriage to steer, as this would have enhanced manoeuvrability on the ground to take advantage of wind direction.

The problem of insufficient power was due to the engine makers, for Frost had calculated that between 20 and 25 hp would be required to lift the machine from the ground but the unit supplied could only sustain a fraction of that. The 5 hp steam engine was built by H.C. Ahrbecker, Son & Hamken of Stamford Street, London, whose business was concerned with the production of lightweight steam engines, launch power plants and similar items, and who were contractors to the Admiralty at that time. The package supplied by the engine builder consisted of a complete power plant to drive Frost's aircraft, and it included all the attachments, levers, connections and so on suitable for the purpose together with a 'once-through', kerosene-fired water-tube boiler. Although the firm was not in the mainstream of steam engine construction in the UK, it did have a good reputation for

Figure 30. Edward Frost adjusting the mechanism of his ornithopter.

power plant was unable to flap the wings with sufficient speed to gain lift. In the end Frost gave up and abandoned the machine. First it was stored in a barn and later it was left out in the open under some trees on the estate to moulder. Apparently it was still in existence as late as 1918, for it was examined by Mr D.G. Marshall who wrote about it in the *Cambridge Independent Press* on 5 July 1929. Power was said to be the only major problem, for the machine was very light – with the boiler/ engine unit installed it only weighed 900 lb, of which about 300 lb accounted for the machinery.

This ornithopter was not the end of the Frost story for, in collaboration with Dr W.F. Hutchinson of Cambridge, Mr C.R. d'Esterre, W.G. Pye Scientific Instrument Makers of Chesterton and the Cambridge Autocar Co., he commenced work on several experimental models based on the same principles as the previous machine in 1902. This work culminated in the production of a second version of the ornithopter which was powered by a 3 hp Kelecom internal combustion engine in 1904. This second version did work after a fashion, for the engine managed to lift the machine bodily into the air at each downstroke to a height of about 2 ft whilst tethered to the ground. It only weighed 232 lb and its power-to-weight ratio was therefore far superior to the 1870 machine.

To the end Mr Frost contended that his 'flexible wing' was the answer to any advance in aeronautics and he was convinced that slow-speed flying was the most important aspect of aviation. It eventually took two types of aircraft to combine his theories – the jump-jet and the helicopter. Unfortunately although Frost was an aspirant 'airman' he remained firmly a 'groundsman'.

Apart from the steam engine in the Shuttleworth Collection, a wing from the later ornithopter survives in the National Collection at the Science Museum in South Kensington, London.

Lawrence Hargrave (1850–1915)

Hargrave was an Englishman who lived in Australia. He began studying aeronautics in the early 1880s and presented twenty-three papers concerning aviation to the Royal Society of New South Wales. His initial experiments were concerned with rubber-powered ornithopters but he also made models driven by compressed air. One of these models, driven by a single-cylinder engine, is depicted in Fig. 32, where it is seen to have wings of greater chord than span and two flapping wings forward of the plane surfaces. All of Hargrave's models showed the same characteristics, and one of his hallmarks was the use of pronounced dihedral. In 1889 he manufactured a three-cylinder

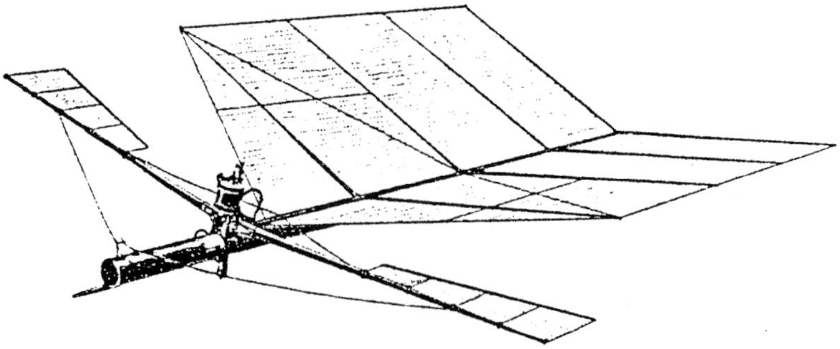

Figure 32. Lawrence Hargrave's single-cylinder compressed-air driven ornithopter model of about 1884.

rotary compressed air engine, the first such machine for use in aviation.

Professor Baranovsky

This Russian professor envisaged the extraordinary machine depicted in fig. 33. It was proposed in St Petersburg in 1883, and consisted of a cylindrical, cigar-shaped, fuselage which contained a 'powerful steam engine' which not only flapped the wings, but also drove three propellers: one at the aft end and two others beneath each wing. The machine was never built but was just another 'flight of the imagination'.

Two other inventors in the nineteenth century patented steam driven-ornithopters but apparently did not make working models. These were

Figure 33. Professor Baranovsky's proposed steam ornithopter.

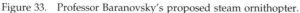

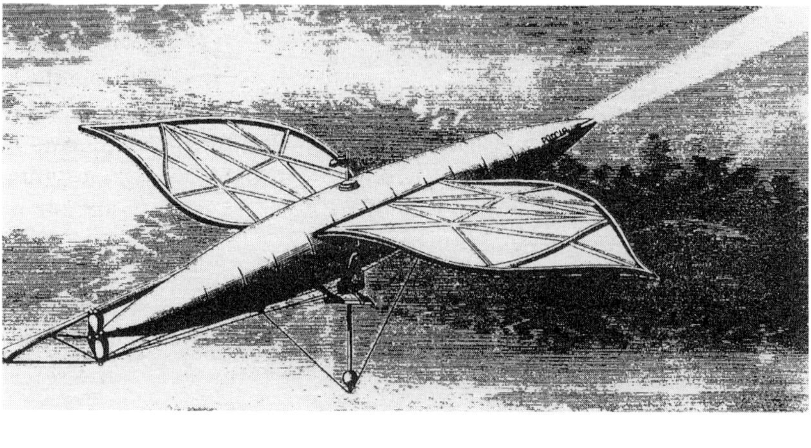

Matthew Boulton with his 'Flying Machine' (Brit. Pat. No. 1005 of 1868), and Henry Middleton who had two patents with the same title (Brit. Pat. Nos. 9725 of 1888, and 21885 of 1891).

Helicopters

During the middle part of the nineteenth century a number of experimenters had some success with rotary wing aircraft driven by steam. The first of these was W.H. Phillips, who built a novel rotating wing model which had rotors turned by jets on their tips by steam generated by the combustion of a mixture of potassium nitrate, charcoal and gypsum. By all accounts this model was successful. Later, in the second half of the twentieth century the 'jet-tip' system became commonplace in helicopters. He was followed by others who dabbled with differing forms of rotating-wing machines.

Vicomte Ponton d'Amecourt

This French nobleman experimented with helicopters made to designs that were set out in his specification, Brit. Pat. No. 1929 of 1861. He constructed several rotary-winged machines, all of which had contra-rotating blades. The first models were powered by clockwork and flew well, but a later one, illustrated in fig. 34, was fitted with a steam engine, and this unit was too heavy, which inhibited the aircraft from flying at all. The rotors produced lift but the engine had insufficient power to enable sustained flight. The principle was correct, however, for when Louis Joseph built a similar machine driven by a clockwork movement if flew well. The name plate on the steam example appears to indicate that Joseph made this one as well, for it reads 'Louis Jsh, Paris'.

From the picture we can see that the steam-driven model was a compact entity with a monotube boiler, possibly of Herreshoff design, at its base; this boiler was surmounted by a twin-cylinder simple steam engine which drove overhung cranks to which a shaft was attached to a pinion which, in turn drove a countershaft having bevel gears to actuate the paddle-like blades in opposing directions. Had a lighter engine with a better power-to-weight ratio been available there is no doubt that this model would have worked.

Gabriel de la Landelle

The interest in helicopters threw up some fantastic ideas, with even Jules Verne proposing a huge ship's hull with an imposing array of rotors mounted on the upper deck.

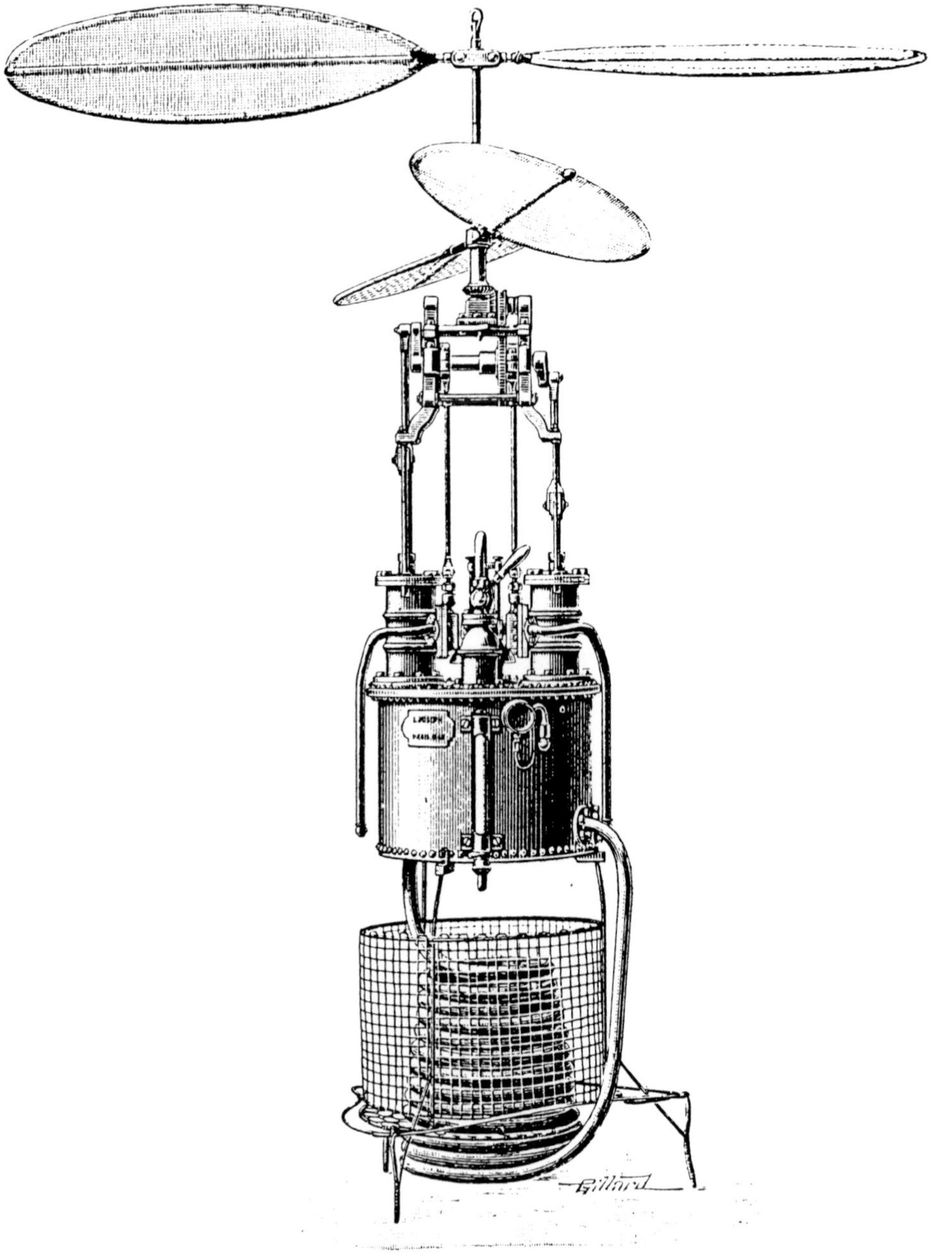

Figure 34. The steam helicopter devised by the Vicomte Gustave de Ponton d'Amecourt.

Figure 35. The extraordinary device proposed by Gabriel de la Landelle in 1863.

However, the most bizarre notion to be put forward at this time was the design of de la Landelle published in 1863 and illustrated in fig. 35. This gargantuan machine was to consist of a hull with a promenade deck housing a steam boiler at its centre, carrying two side planes or wings, empennages fore and aft, and two vertical masts each fitted with four sets of rotors. This absurd 'ship of the sky' was totally impractical and it goes without saying that no attempt was ever made to build it. It is interesting to note, however, that it was de la Landelle who invented the word 'aviation' which has come into general use around the world.

Wilhelm von Achenbach

Another monstrous proposal was published in 1874 when this German inventor described a huge helicopter driven by steam which had some interesting features.

The machine had a steam engine and a boiler in the centre of the fuselage which drove a vertical shaft to rotate the large sail-like rotors

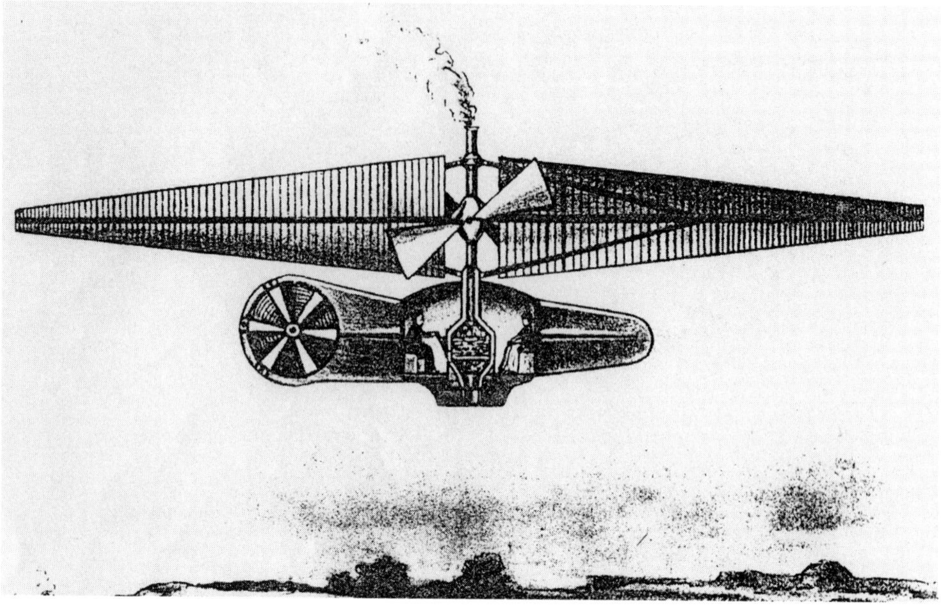

Figure 36. The large helicopter design of Achenbach (Courtesy of the Helicopter Museum, Locking).

and provided translation to forward thrust via a gearbox to a two-bladed propeller (see fig. 36). An ingenious part of the design was the provision of a six-bladed 'anti-torque' rotor to prevent rotation of the fuselage. It is believed that Achenbach was the first pioneer to realize the importance of this item in helicopter construction; he also fitted a rudder and used a passenger as a counterweight. This machine was never built.

Dieuaide and Castel

Between the 1860s and the late 1870s more work was done in the field of helicopters, including two interesting machines which are believed to have become airborne in some way or another. In 1877 a gentleman by the name of Dieuaide experimented with a rotary-winged, steam-powered machine with contra-rotating blades similar to d'Amecourt's. In the same year, another Frenchman, P. Castel, is known to have built the compressed air helicopter shown in fig. 37. This model had four sets of blades, probably contra-rotating, driven off a bevel-geared countershaft. This machine was fed with air from a ground-based compressor using a flexible pipe; it did get aloft but it soon came down and crashed into a wall.

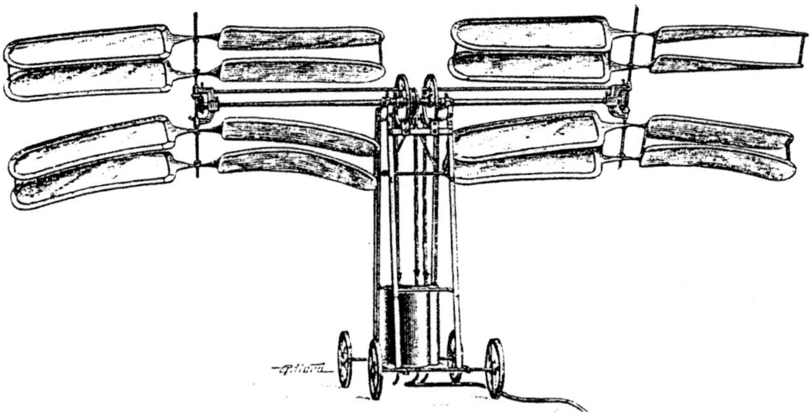

Figure 37. The helicopter built by P. Castel in 1877. It was fed with compressed air from a plant located on the ground.

Enrico Forlanini

This Italian is credited with manufacturing the first helicopter to make a sustained flight; whether or not it was controlled is open to conjecture. It was operated by a novel method, for when in flight there was no fire. The outline of the machine is illustrated in fig. 38. The sphere beneath the two sets of contra-rotating blades was the boiler and this element was heated by means of a fire on the ground until superheated steam was produced, at which point the blade began to rotate and the craft became airborne. Forlanini's engine produced ¼ hp and it worked at 160 psi; weighing 6 lb its power-to-weight ratio was 24 lb to the horse-power. This craft is preserved in the Museo Technica di Leonardo da Vinci in Milan.

J. Melikov

The 'hélicoptère à vapeur d'ether' that was proposed by Melikov, an emigré Russian working in France, in 1879 (see fig. 39) was a strange device – a cross between a powered parachute and a helicopter, notable inasmuch as it proposed gas turbine propulsion.

The machine consisted of a hollowed 'spearhead' which was intended to 'screw' the equipage into the air and to act as a parachute to allow it to descent after flight.

The most interesting part of the invention was the engine, which was novel for its period; it was designed to provide power both for ascension and for forward motion. The power unit was described by Melikov as being a 'gas turbine consisting of eight curved chambers, into which charges of ether vapour mixed with air were to be

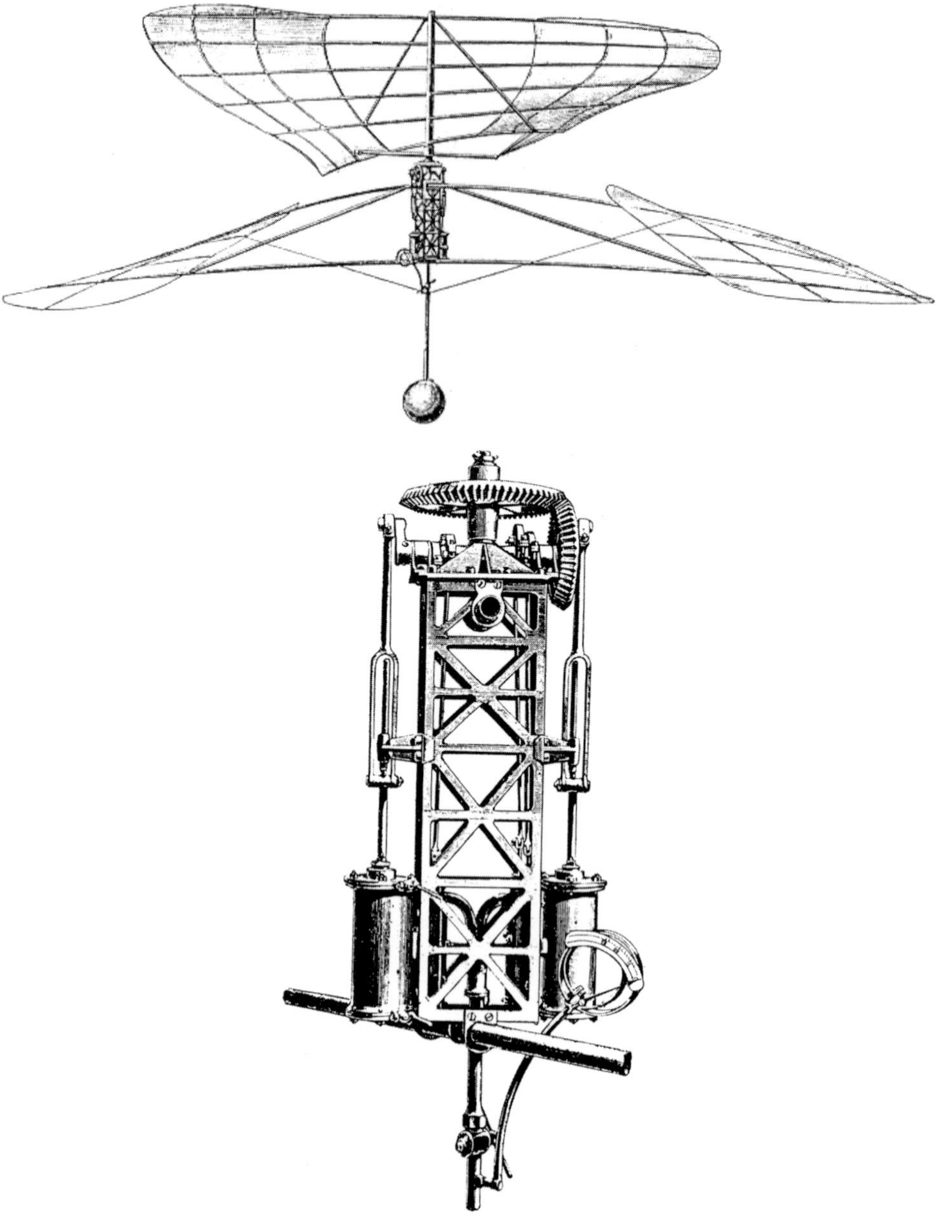

Figure 38. The successful steam-driven helicopter built in Italy by Enrico Forlanini in 1877. The vertically mounted twin-cylinder engine was similar to that used by the Vicomte Ponton d'Amecourt and, again used overhung cranks and bevel gearing. Forlanini went on to be a successful airship constructor in Italy.

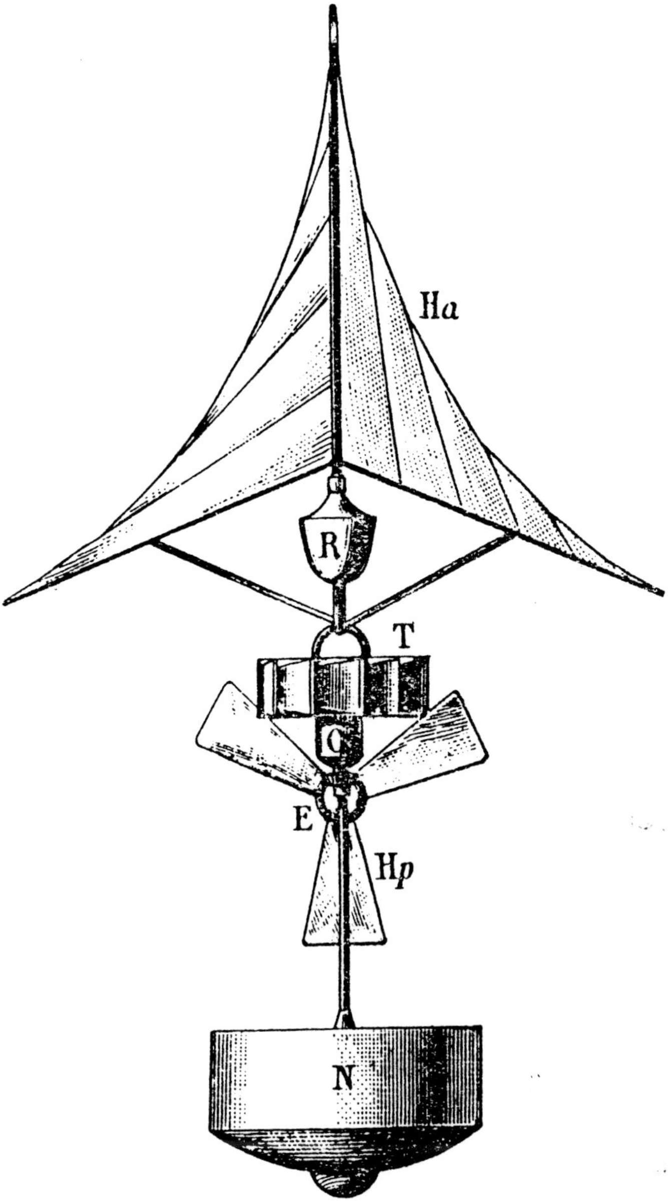

Figure 39. Line drawing of the curious helicopter proposed by J. Melikov in 1879. The key to the components is as follows: Ha, lifting airscrew; Hp, propulsive airscrew; E, wheel and pinion gearing; T, reaction turbine; R, reservoir of ether; C, explosion chamber containing a mixture of air and ether; N, nacelle.

successively exploded by an electric spark, the expanding charge providing the power'. The turbine was mounted on a shaft which directly revolved the lifting airscrew whilst a wheel and pinion gearing system rotated the propeller to give forward thrust. It is included here because in the specification, Melikov mentioned that steam could be an alternative source of power.

Other inventors who produced specifications at this time were Philip Masey (Brit. Pat. No. 412 of 1868), Robert Courtemanche (Brit. Pat. No. 2031 of 1871) and John Cave, who described a compressed-air helicopter in Brit. Pat. No. 140 of 1875.

Composite aircraft

There appears to have been only one composite aircraft made during the middle of the nineteenth century: the 'Avitor', which was constructed by a San Francisco publisher named Frederick Marriot. This machine, which was part balloon and part powered glider, appears to have been an element of a dubious stock promotion scheme. At first a large model named the *Avitor Hermes Jr.* was made in 1868–9 and a company was formed to construct a full-sized version. This venture was named The Aerial Steam Navigation Company and it was founded with a declared capital of $1 million. All sorts of publicity stunts were arranged, including a poetry competition to promote the sale of stock which was won by Bret Harte, a popular writer of the day.

Figure 40. An illustration of Frederick Marriott's composite machine as published in the promotional literature of the Aerial Steam Navigation Company in 1869.

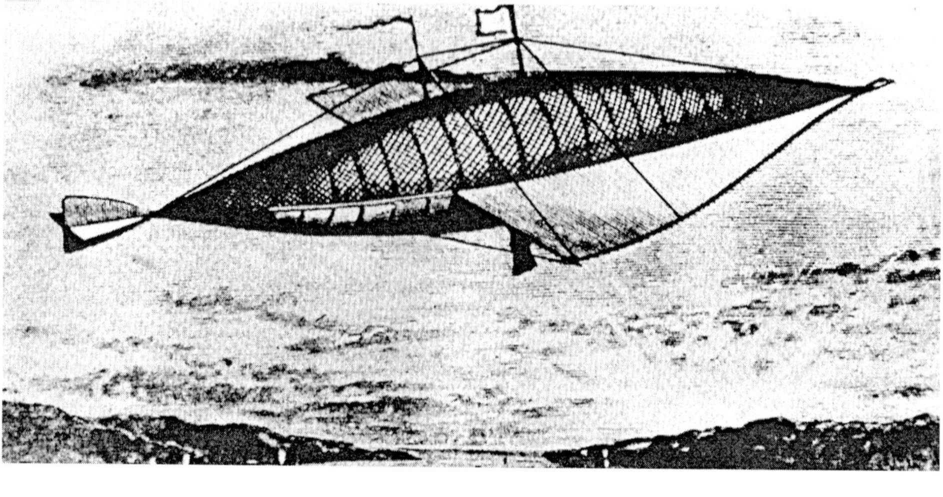

This poem was entitled 'Avitor (An Aerial Retrospect)' and it parodied Longfellow's 'Excelsior'. A drawing of the machine (see fig. 40) was included in the promotional literature and this illustration is very near in design to the actual model that was made and flown.

Marriott's model was demonstrated successfully in July 1869 in a field near San Francisco, where it made a ten-minute tethered flight, being led around by its inventor; it was the first aircraft to leave the ground in a controlled and sustained flight in the USA. It has been stated that it was later flown on several occasions; it was certainly one of the first aircraft to be photographed for there is a stereopticon slide in existence depicting it aloft. Unfortunately there are apparently no details of the power unit of its boiler on record. The full-sized version was never built. Marriot was the same person who was involved with Henson's 'Aerial Transit Company' of 1843.

CHAPTER THREE

The Period of Scientific Achievement

Following on from the experiments of the mid-1800s where, as we have seen, all types of aircraft were considered including airships, ornithopters and helicopters, the fixed-wing heavier-than-air configuration became the main focus of attention at the end of the nineteenth century. During the last fifteen years of the century six major pioneers and several minor players concerned themselves with steam-driven aircraft, with varying degrees of success. They came from all over the world – Russia, France, Germany, the UK and the USA, and the aircraft they built ranged from the delicate model made by Professor Samuel Langley in 1896 to the monstrous creation that ran upon rails that was constructed by Sir Hiram Maxim.

Alexandr Fedorovich Mozhaiskii (1825–90)

Whilst the career of this Russian naval officer has been well documented, his claims in aviation have been the subject of scepticism and even ridicule over the years, owing to conflicting reports that were published by the Soviet propaganda machine during the Stalinist era. In an effort to convince the world of the prowess of Russian inventors and scientists by claiming 'firsts' in nearly every branch of science and technology, these propagandists made a laughing stock of some very able pioneers. The truth concerning Mozhaiskii has now been revealed, and it would appear that he was, indeed, an important figure in the course of aviation history, who was working along the right lines to achieve flight.

He was born on the 9 March 1825, in a place named as Rochensalm in modern-day Finland, the son of an officer in the Russian navy. In

1836, he entered the Navy as a cadet, and by 1841 he was seconded to the Baltic Fleet; by the middle of 1853, now with the rank of lieutenant, he joined the frigate *Diana*. He rose to the rank of captain.

Alexandr Fedorovich Mozhaiskii

Mozhaiskii's interest in flight started in 1856 and he is known to have conducted a programme of experiments before building a full-sized aeroplane. At first he busied himself with the observation of bird flights, (as did most of the early pioneers). Twenty years later, in 1876, he was in St Petersburg to conduct some experiments; one of which was a man-carrying kite towed behind a horse-drawn vehicle, and later some successful models powered by clockwork. Clockwork was a favourite mechanism for providing power in aircraft models in the nineteenth century and several inventors had used it successfully, amongst them Pierre Julien, a clockmaker from Villejuif, who made a model airship in 1850 that inspired Henri Giffard. As we have seen, the Vicomte Ponton d'Amecourt used this power source, as did Felix du Temple, who made the first model aircraft to fly properly. As a result of the successful testing of his clockwork models Mozhaiskii approached the Russian War Ministry for monetary assistance and was given a grant of 3,000 roubles, of which 1,000 roubles were made available immediately to continue model experiments using both clockwork and steam as motive power.

In February 1887 Mozhaiskii formulated his 'Programme of Experiments Involving Model Apparatus', part of which concerned research into flight and part power sources and control surfaces. As he continued his research his capital began to dwindle and he wished, somewhat prematurely, to progress to the full-sized prototype; he estimated the cost precisely at 18,895 roubles and 45 kopeks! His original proposals for the machine had included the use of a Brayton oil engine which had been invented by George Bailey Brayton in the USA. The Brayton Ready Motor had been invented in 1872 and it was put into production a year later at the Exeter Machine Works in New Hampshire. It was a double-acting, two-stroke unit designed to burn oil of 0.85 sg, but it was more suited to a land application than an aeronautical one. In the end Mozhaiskii abandoned this form of prime mover in favour of steam, despite the fact that the weight of the steam plant with all of its associated auxiliaries might jeopardize his chances of becoming airborne.

His proposals for the airframe comprised a monoplane with a wingspan of 75 ft. The main plane was fabric covered and had an area of 3,800 sq. ft, it was braced with wires from two kingposts stepped into the boat-style fuselage/cockpit (see fig. 41). The drawings for this machine (see figs. 42 and 43) show the general arrangement, with one tractor propeller at the nose and two pusher propellers at the trailing edge of the wings near the cruciform tail unit; however in the final design the rear propellers were moved to cut-outs about one-third of the distance from the leading edge of each wing.

Having outlined his proposals, Mozhaiskii went in search of funds with which to continue his research and development. In 1878 he managed to obtain a small personal material grant of 600 roubles from the War Ministry Engineering Section, but this was insufficient for his needs. He applied to the Naval Ministry in the following year and gained the sum of 2,500 roubles for a visit to the USA in search of a suitable power unit. In the event this proved to be abortive for he could find no engine with the power-to-weight ratio that was deemed to be necessary to lift a heavier-than-air machine from the ground. He was

Figure 41. Method of rigging to kingposts of the Mozhaiskii aeroplane.

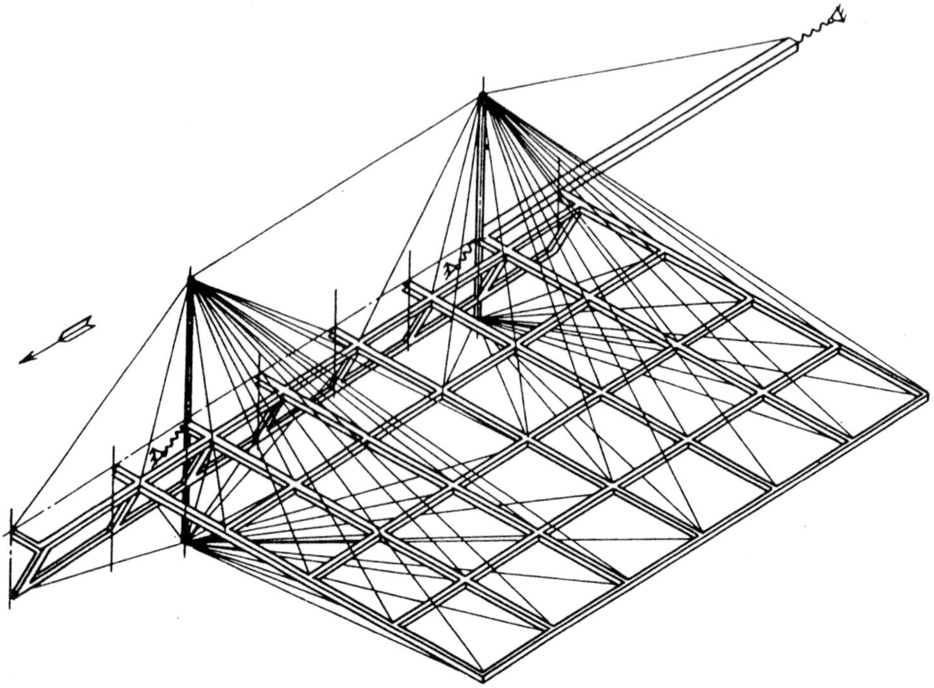

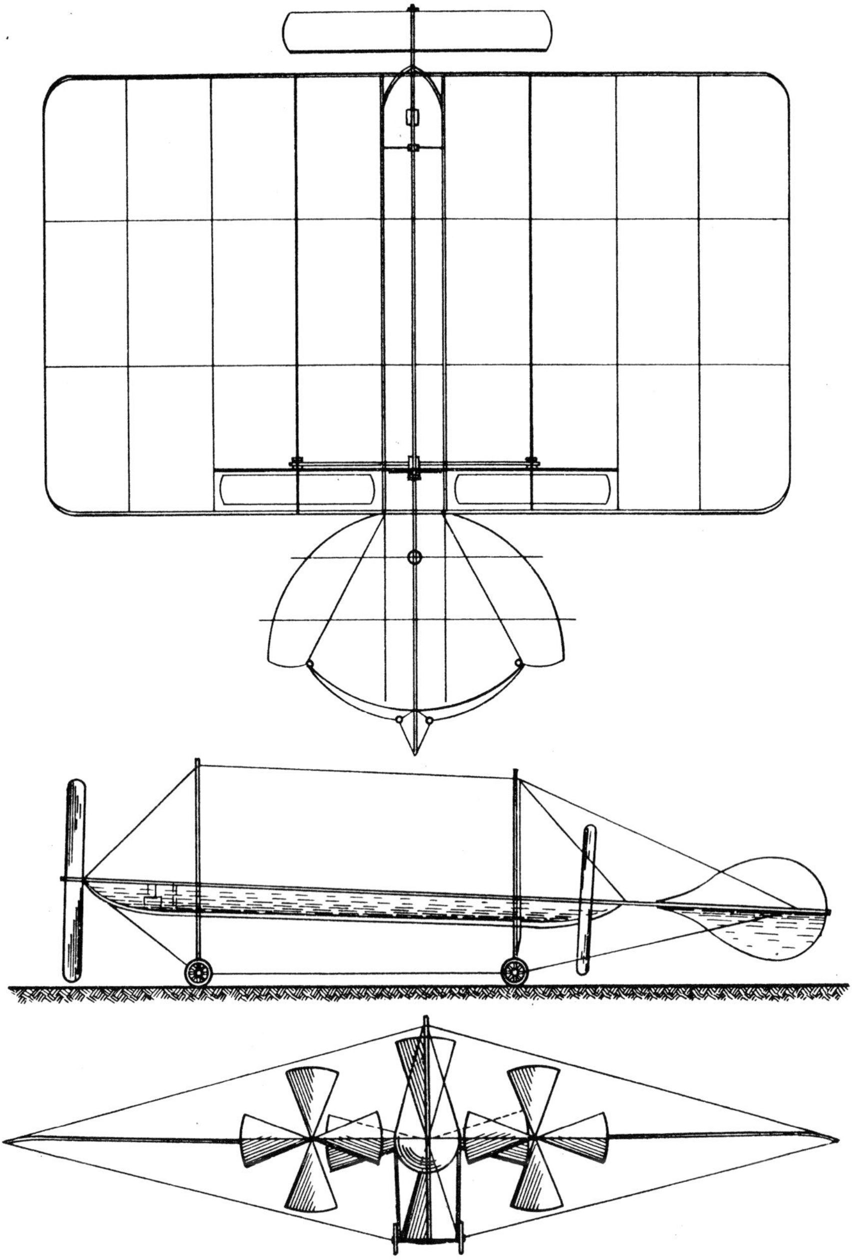

Figure 42. The original configuration of the monoplane constructed by Alexandr Mozhaiskii.

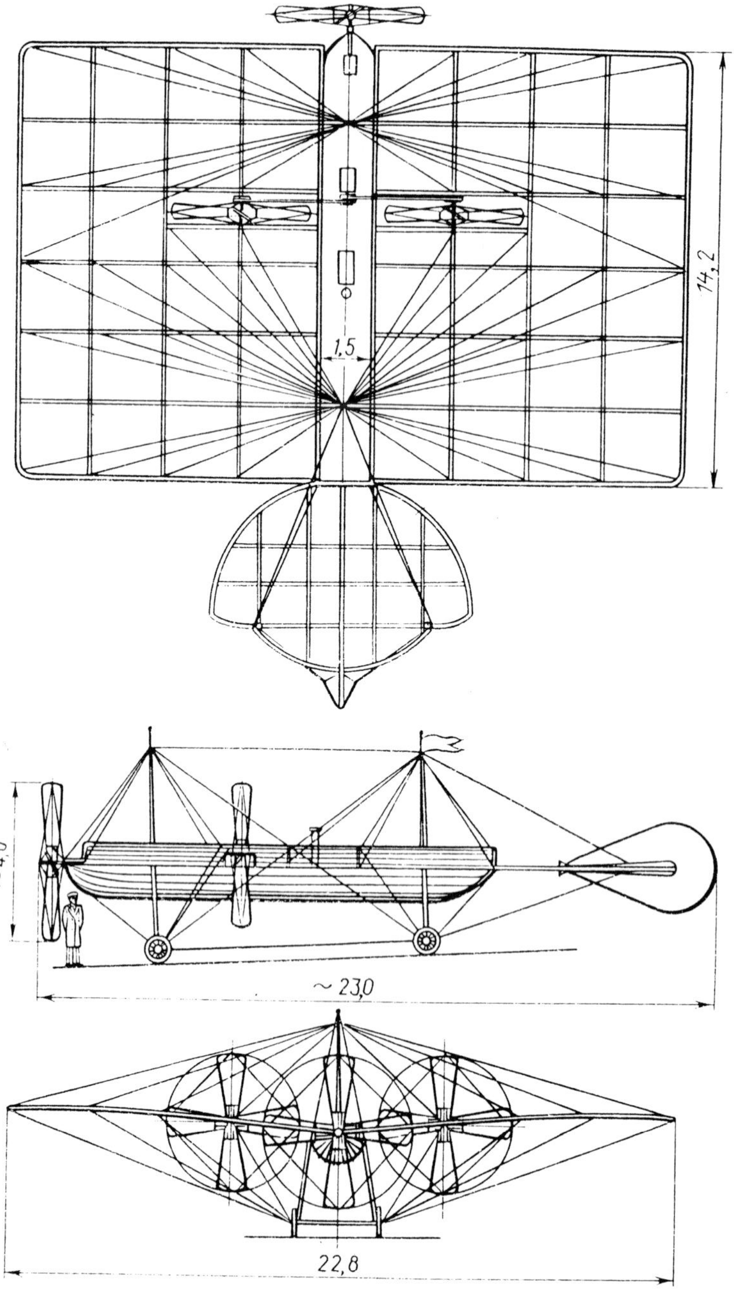

Figure 43. The revised layout of the Mozhaiskii steam monoplane.

therefore forced to turn to steam power. He visited the UK and ended up at the doors of Ahrbecker, Son & Hamkens, the firm that had made the engine for the Frost ornithopter in the 1870s. He ordered two steam engines, one of 20 hp (see fig. 44) and one of 10 hp, together with a tubular boiler and a condenser, and these were despatched to Russia in May 1881.

Once again, he was running short of money, and another request, this time for a grant of 5,000 roubles was turned down. However, three leading aristocrats, Prince Oldenberg, Graf Vorontsov-Dashkov and General Skobelev, came to his rescue and provided 2,800 roubles in time for him to start construction of his craft. In the summer of 1881 the manufacture of the components for the flying machine was begun at the Baltiisky Promashlennya Zavod under the direction of its principal, M.I. Kazi.

Mozhaiskii had applied for a patent to cover his work in June 1880 and this was subsequently granted as Privilegia No. 103 of 1881, the first such protection in Russia for a flying machine. The citation stated: 'Issued by the Department of Trade and Manufacture in the Year 1881 to Captain 1st Rank Alexandr Mozhaiskii for Aeronautical Equipment.' It went on to say, 'Captain 1st Rank Alexandr Mozhaiskii resident of Saint Petersburg on 4 June 1880 has applied to the Department of Trade and Manufacture for a petition to deliver a *priveligia* for Aeronautical Equipment.' The patent then went on to describe the type of apparatus that Mozhaiskii proposed to build. One of the conditions of this grant of letters was that the project should be completed by the summer of 1883.

During the early part of 1882 Mozhaiskii was given permission to work in the grounds of the Guard Force of the St Petersburg Military District at Krashnoe Selo; here he erected temporary premises and construction of the aeroplane began in the summer. Work went slowly and it was still not ready by January 1883. In July Mozhaiskii indicated that it had been completed but requested that further modifications be carried out, apparently the movement of the hind propellers from the trailing edge of the wings to a new position within the cut-outs amidships. At this time all three airscrews were of the same diameter, with the 10 hp engine powering the nose one and the 20 hp unit connected to both of the amidships propellers (see figs. 42 and 43). Some tests were carried out, as it was 'propelled on a sloping ramp' but it did not fly so presumably these were just pre-flight checks to determine the engine performance etc.

By the end of 1883 Mozhaiskii had again been reduced to an impecunious state and he applied to the Tsar for a grant of 2,800 roubles

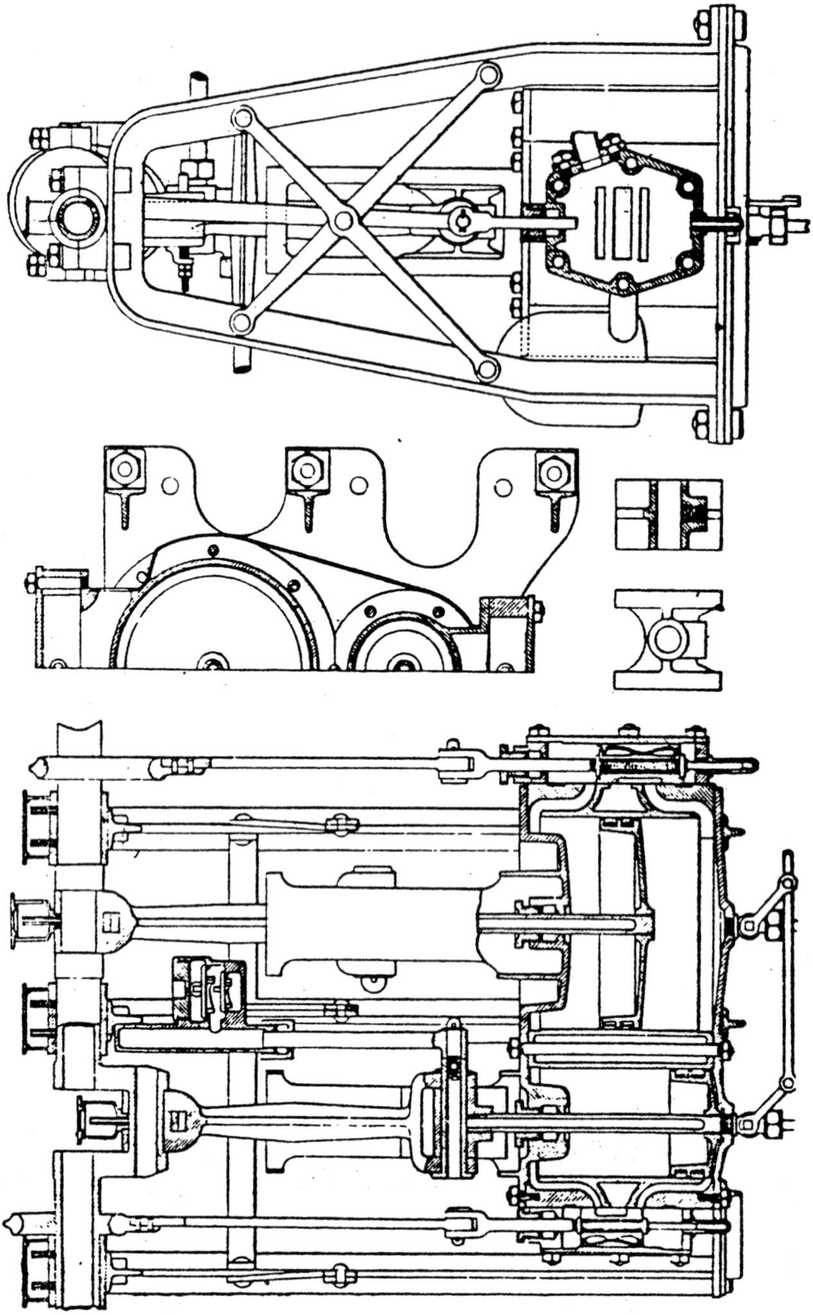

Figure 44. The 20 hp steam engine supplied to Alexandr Mozhaiskii by Ahrbecker, Son & Hamkens. (Drawing by courtesy of *Engineering*.)

to complete the machine and carry out the final tests prior to the flight. This application was refused and in October 1884 it was stated that experiments conducted so far were unsuccessful due to 'outside causes' (lack of money perhaps!). More applications for finance were made to the War Ministry and these were duly turned down despite Mozhaiskii's plea that money was necessary for the completion of the machine and the carrying out of tests, the scope of which, he suggested, could be determined by a commission after due examination of the aircraft.

It appears that one attempt was made to fly the Mozhaiskii aeroplane, probably in July 1885; whether or not the machine became airborne is uncertain but it has been reported that it was directionally unstable and crashed, causing damage to its wings.

The stories of the pilot Golubev and the ski-jump style or ramp down which the attempted flight is said to have been made, may have been fiction, but it does seem that the craft possibly became airborne for a distance of between 65 and 100 ft. At the end of 1885, after the flight attempt, Mozhaiskii removed the British engines as they did not have sufficient power to maintain the aeroplane in flight, and, in October 1886 he ordered two larger copies of the 20 hp unit from the Obukovsky Zavod in an effort to boost available power to 60 hp. However, these modifications were never completed, for the second engine was not finished until after his death on 20 March 1890.

Another mystery concerns the offer by Mozhaiskii's sons to sell the remains of the aeroplane to the War Ministry for the sum of 20,000 roubles following his death. The Ministry declined to purchase the machine and it subsequently disappeared without trace! The British engines, which had been removed for safe keeping to the Baltisky Zavod, were destroyed in a fire on 17 October 1895.

The exact configuration of the Mozhaiskii aeroplane has not been fully recorded, though drawings of the period and other archive material do give a relatively accurate representation of the machine. From these sources a model has been made, which is displayed in a flying attitude in the House of Aviation in Moscow; there is also a similar, but much smaller, model in the Aeronautical Gallery of the Narodni Vekhers Museum in Prague. The two generally known layouts of the Mozhaiskii flying machine are shown in figs. 42 and 43, whilst a reconstructed model designed for tests in Moscow during 1979 to 1981 is shown in the drawing in fig. 45. The dimensions for the full-sized machine (which are only approximate, for different sources give different figures), are as follows: wingspan 74 ft 10 in; length overall 75 ft 6 in; width of fuselage 5 ft; chordal dimension 46 ft 7 in; the weight

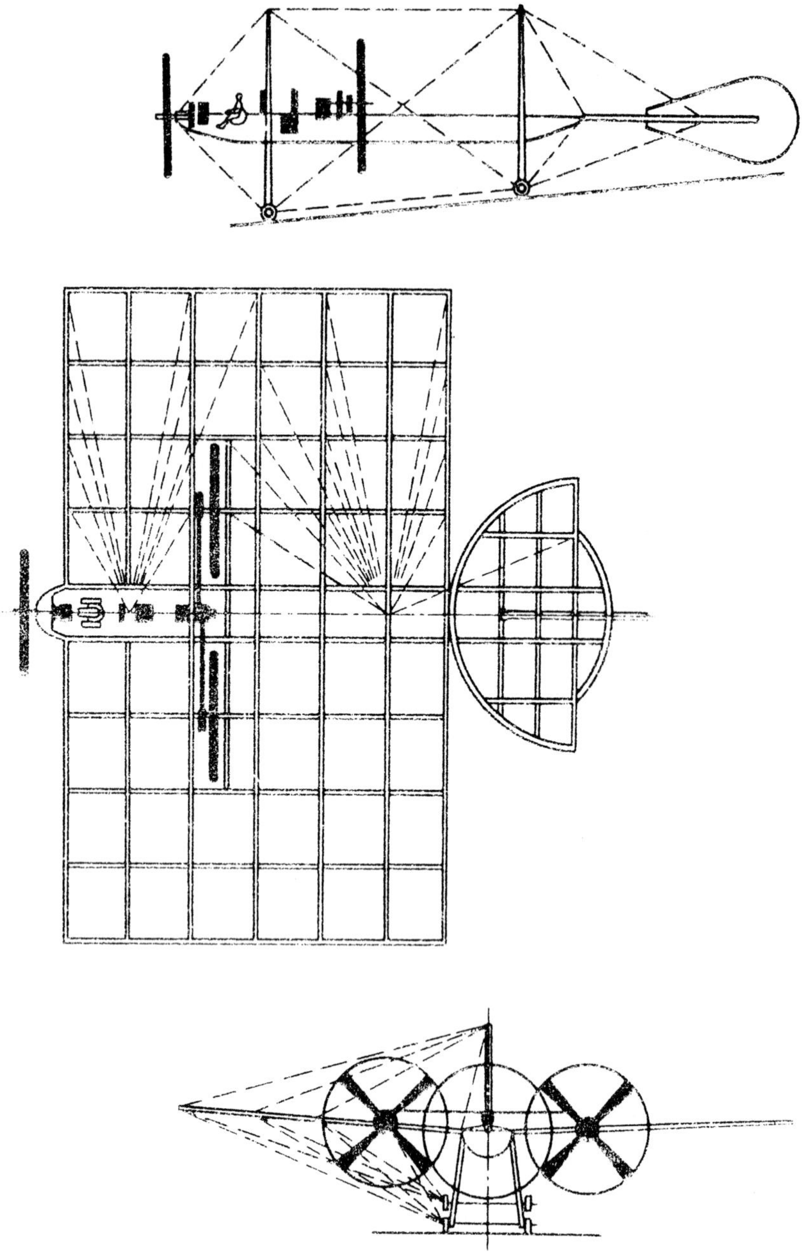

Figure 45. Drawing showing a reconstructed model of the Mozhaiskii aeroplane as used for tests in 1979 at TsAGI in Moscow.

of the machine has been given variously as 2,055 lb and 2,866 lb. It may be deduced from these measurements that the aeroplane was of considerable size (see colour section page 6).

The power units supplied by Ahrbecker, Son & Hamkens were of the compound double-acting type and, as mentioned before, were of 10 and 20 hp. The dimensions and other details of these engines are as follows:

Engine type	2-cylinder compound	2-cylinder compound
HP	10	20
Bores	2½ and 5 in	3¾ and 7½ in
Stroke	3½ in	5 in
Working pressure	190 psi	190 psi
Rotational speed	450 rpm	300 rpm
Engine weight	63 lb	105 lb
Boiler type	Tubular (possibly Herreshoff pattern)	
Weight of boiler	142 lb	
Total weight	Both engines and boilers 310 lb	
Power-to-weight ratio	10.33 lb per hp	

A line drawing of the 20 hp unit was published in *Engineering* the 6 May 1881 and is reproduced in fig. 44.

Some experiments conducted at the Central Aerodynamics and Hydrodynamics Institute (TsAGI) between 1979 and 1981, show some estimates concerning the probable performance of the Mozhaiskii machine. The tests were made on a 1/20 scale model in the Institute's T-102 wind tunnel at velocities of 44.7, 67.1 and 89.4 mph using four different styles of airscrew. The conclusions that were drawn from these experiments were as follows:

> *Mozhaiskii's flying machine, in calm weather, from a level surface with the limited power available, could not reach the take-off velocity of 12.8 metres per second* [28.6 mph]. *A maximum speed of only 7 metres per second* [15.6 mph] *was permissible .... These calculations and experiments have established that the power available was insufficient to enable sustained level flight of the machine.*

Despite the results of these tests Alexandr Mozhaiskii was a true pioneer, well to the fore of flight technology in the last years of the nineteenth century. Some of his theories were in advance of other pioneers, such as Sir Hiram Maxim, who were his contemporaries. As it stands, his machine only possessed one-third of the power necessary to achieve sustained flight at its weight; whether or not 60 hp steam engines could have got it aloft is uncertain, as its controllability was

Figure 46. A representation of A.F. Mozhaiskii's monoplane about to take off down an inclined wooden ramp.

questionable. Nevertheless, if he had lived on, it is possible that he may have outdone Clément Ader in being the first person to take off under power in a heavier-than-air craft.

J.-C. Pompien Piraud

In 1879 this French experimenter built a steam driven ornithopter which apparently lifted itself off the ground during a test 'flight' at Grand Camp, Lyons, before the steam plant exploded to destroy the machine! In 1882 he tried again with another steam ornithopter (see fig. 47) which used 'bat-like' wings to provide lift. It seemed that no definite results arose from his efforts.

Whilst he did little to advance the received wisdom of the time, however, he did record his observations in some considerable detail, in book form, on his efforts to construct a workable flying machine. This was published in Paris in 1903 (see the Bibliography).

A. Goupil

Goupil was another French engineer who built and tested a monoplane glider which held against a wind of 12 mph and was capable of lifting two men off the ground. It had a wing area of 290 sq. ft, a 20 ft wing span, and a length of 26 ft. It was flown in 1883.

The following year, Goupil initiated a steam aeroplane project which he entitled *'Aeroplane à Vapeur de 2,000 k'*. Presumably the reference to '2,000 k' related to its proposed weight. It was an ambitious idea, as can be seen from figs. 48 and 49. Note the 'streamline' fuselage or body, the concave, elliptical wings reminiscent of those fitted to the Supermarine

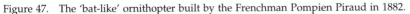

Figure 47. The 'bat-like' ornithopter built by the Frenchman Pompien Piraud in 1882.

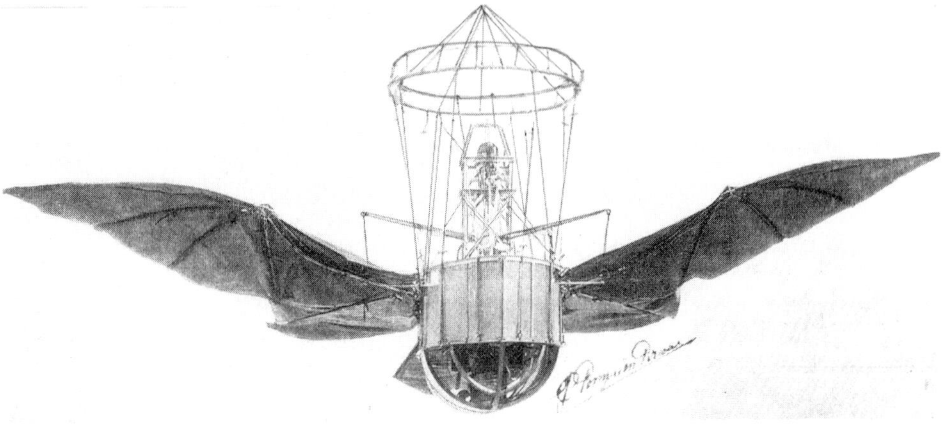

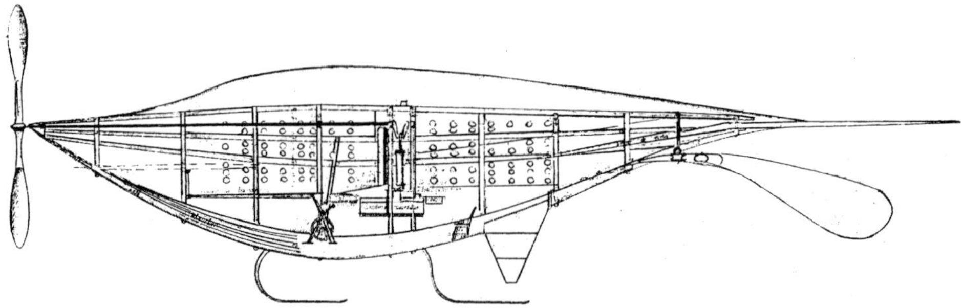

Figure 48. Sectional side view of the *'Aeroplane à Vapeur de 2000k'* proposed by A. Goupil.

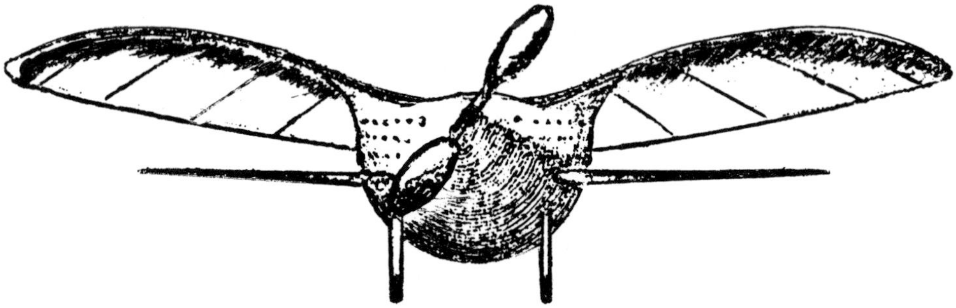

Figure 49. Head-on view of Goupil's proposed steam monoplane.

'Spitfire', with a small span but deep roots and a quadruple skid pattern undercart. In the sectional view of the fuselage (fig. 48), the steam cylinder is inverted and the airscrew shaft is directly attached to the crankshaft; there is no hint of the style of valve gear and it has not been recorded whether the engine was single- or double-acting. The boiler was designed to be fitted below the cylinder. In front of the power source there was a winch arrangement to control the various aerofoil surfaces.

Goupil was one of the few inventors of his time to recognize the need for ailerons and understand their use, for he proposed to install two rigid planes mounted either side at the front of the aircraft which were capable of independent movement in two planes. He called these 'regulators', and along with the tailplane and rudder they were to be actuated by the winching system. They could be moved in unison to achieve upward or downward flight but if they moved independently and in opposing directions Goupil said that they could provide directional assistance to the rudder – it is thought that he was the first pioneer to recognize this fact. The pilot's seat was in some way connected to the winch system and a form of 'auto-control' was possible by the pilot swinging the seat to operate the regulators. The V-shaped body projecting downwards behind the rear skids was a combined entrance and goods store.

Whilst the craft was an esoteric creation, it shows that the general configuration of the aeroplane was known in the 1880s and that the use of ailerons, tailplane surfaces and rudders were needed adjuncts to just wings and body. It has been thought that Mozhaiskii also recognized the value of ailerons though he did not use them in his machine.

Victor Tatin

Following his experiments with a compressed-air model in 1879 (see chapter 2) Victor Tatin, in collaboration with Professor Charles Richet, built and tested a model steam aeroplane of considerable size, demonstrating that Tatin was a notable figure in the quest for heavier-than-air flight.

Whilst his 1879 model did fly for a limited period in the round the pole mode, the results of the flight added little to the knowledge of the day and were inconclusive. However, with the help of Richet he sought to demonstrate the practicability of a similar design, but in a larger format. Whereas the original model weighed only 4 lb, the 1890 machine had a total weight of 73 lb with 24 lb accounting for the steam power unit. The air reservoir of the 1879 model, which was made from a spiral steel strip rolled up into a tube and secured by 1,800 rivets, formed the fuselage, but in the later attempt a boat-shaped 'power car', a wooden framework covered with canvas, housed the engine and boiler (see fig. 50). From this 'power car' a shaft ran longitudinally to drive both tractor and pusher airscrews located at either end. The whole equipage was a neat and well-thought-out design which exhibited many factors now known to be necessary in aircraft construction; for

Figure 50. The Tatin-Richet steam monoplane of 1890.

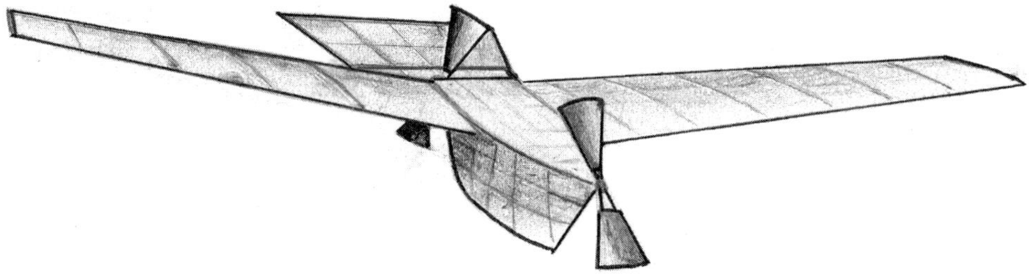

example, the seven frames in each wing were made as an elliptical section, whilst solid spars ran the length of the wings to provide an element of strength. These wings also had an angle of dihedral of about 10 degrees; with a wingspan of 21 ft 8 in the surface area worked out at 86 sq. ft. One thing lacking was a vertical surface for steerage.

The aeroplane was initially tested at Cap de La Hève in 1890. It was launched into the air down an inclined runway 46 yds long which had a slight elevation at the bottom. At first the machine went well but the tailplane became twisted and the craft crashed into the sea beneath the cliffs. It was repaired and in 1896 and 1897 a further three flights were made in the Giens harbour area but each one ended in a stall, with the aircraft sliding back into the sea; nevertheless a level flight of some 150 yds was achieved in this series of tests. It is not known what became of the 1890 aeroplane but the 1879 model is now preserved in the Musée de l'Air at Le Bourget, Paris.

Horatio Frederick Phillips (1845–1926)

This pioneer was one of the more important contributors to aviation science during the last years of the nineteenth and the early ones of the twentieth century. He is mostly known for his research into aerofoil sections and high aspect-ratio wing formations. He started by experimenting with hydrofoils, and his work has formed the basis for modern aerofoil technology. He filed two patents which revealed his complete understanding of the science of lift using a plane surface: 'Wings with slightly thickened leading edge, so curved on the top surface that a vacuum is produced' (Brit. Pat. No. 13768 of 1884) and 'Wing Sections of Increased Lift' (Brit. Pat. No. 13311 of 1891). These two inventions referred to a system of wing planes arranged one upon the other in the manner of a venetian blind, the hallmark of Phillips's aircraft.

He had dabbled with helicopters driven by steam similar to the machine built by the Vicomte Ponton d'Amécourt in the 1860s but as with the French craft, the weight was too great for lift-off. After examining the performance of controlled box kites Phillips went on to perfect the 'Phillips entry' system as outlined in the above specifications. A further patent, Brit. Pat. No. 20277 of 1891 entitled 'Aerial Machines and Vehicles' described the application of his system to a specific aeroplane.

Using all his patent specifications Phillips went on to demonstrate their effectiveness with a full-sized unmanned aircraft which was used in tethered tests around a 200 ft wooden track at Harrow in 1893 (see fig. 51). This craft weighed 416 lb, including a deadweight payload of

Figure 51. The strange 'test-rig' flying machine demonstrated by Horatio Phillips at Harrow in 1893.

56 lb. The machine was fitted with a three-wheeled frame which supported the wing/aerofoil system and a 6 hp steam engine which drove a two-bladed paddle-like propeller. The 'venetian blind' arrangement had ten upright members and fifty 'wings' or 'sustainers' as Phillips called them. These 'sustainers' had a span of about 19 ft and a chord of only 1½ in. Although this machine was not designed to fly it did lift off for a distance of about 150 ft at a height of some 3 ft.

Continuing from this steam-powered prototype, Phillips went on to be a successful aeronaut during the Edwardian period. He investigated vertical take-off and landing (VTOL) technology and he became well known for his 'multi-plane' style of aircraft of the pre-First World War era. These aeroplanes were the Phillips I of 1904 and the Phillips II of 1907, both of which were fitted with petrol engines. The latter craft is thought to be the first manned heavier-than-air machine to fly in England.

Clément Ader (1841–1925)

Ader was probably the most contentious figure (apart from Gustave Whitehead) in early aviation. He and others made claims and counterclaims which have obscured his true worth as the first person to take off in a powered heavier-than-air machine. It has definitely been established that he left the ground in his steam-driven aircraft, the *Éole,* at about 1600 hrs on 9 October 1890, from level terrain in the grounds of a château at Armainvilliers. His other claims to flight in 1897 with another aeroplane, the *Avion III,* have been proved to be spurious, despite a monument to that effect at Satory, the location of the alleged episode. The full story of his exploits can be found in Charles H. Gibbs-Smith's book 'Clément Ader – His Flight Claims and his Place in History'.

Ader was born at Muret, near Toulouse in the south of France, and he became an inventive, self-taught engineer whose work in telecommunications in the 1880s in Paris is well known. He became interested in aviation during the 1870s, and in 1873 constructed a large 'bird', using feathers from geese, which he tested with some success, to achieve lift in the tethered mode. Some ten years later, he commenced the building of his original aeroplane, the *Éole* (the god of the winds), which took from 1882 to 1890 to complete. On 11 August 1890 he was granted letters patent for an aircraft that was essentially the *Éole* (Brevet d'Invention No. 205155 of 1890). It was a 'bat-like' creation which did not reflect the technology of the day (see fig 52). It had neither elevator nor rudder and had single-surface wings with a steep camber; it appears that Ader took no heed of earlier individuals in the

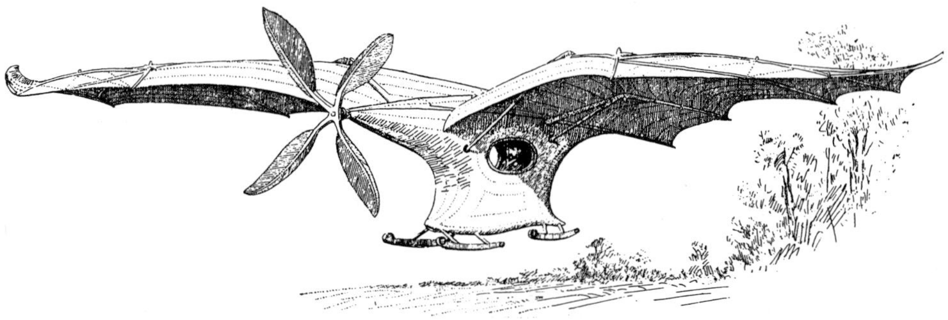

Figure 52. Clément Ader's *Éole* in flight. Note that in this illustration no fuselage mounted condenser is shown. (Originally published in *L'Illustration*, 20 June 1891.)

field such as Henson, Penaud, Tatin and Phillips, and he produced what has been described as a 'freak'. Notwithstanding all of this, he did make a successful take-off, although the subsequent 'flight' of about 165 ft was not sustained or controlled. It is interesting to note that, in 1891, Carl Steiger drew up a plan of an aircraft that would not have looked out of place in the 1930s but apparently Ader was not aware of this design.

The *Éole*, which is shown in detail in Fig. 53, was a complicated piece of equipment which had a system of rods and joints to create a number of actions culminating in a 'swing-wing' movement which was controlled by several hand-cranks and foot pedals. The 'swing-wing' activity was controlled from the cockpit by a hand-crank which had to be turned many times to cause any alteration in position, whilst another crank varied the camber in each wing independently. A further crank-operated system increased or decreased the wing area; the wings could also be completely folded up. Needless to say, the pilot did not have sufficient hands to operate all of these controls simultaneously and to attend to the engine settings at the same time so presumably many of the functions were pre-set before any flight was attempted. The angles of incidence of the wings to enable one to be elevated and the other depressed were controlled by two foot pedals. Altogether there were six hand-cranks, two foot pedals and the engine throttle in the overall control system. The wings were described as being of 'bat-form, single-surface; low aspect-ratio; with extreme "canopied" curvature, i.e. a chord-wise and span-wise curvature; could be folded for storage'.

The 20 hp steam plant of Ader's own design was the best part of the aeroplane, for it was apparently very well made, being extremely light

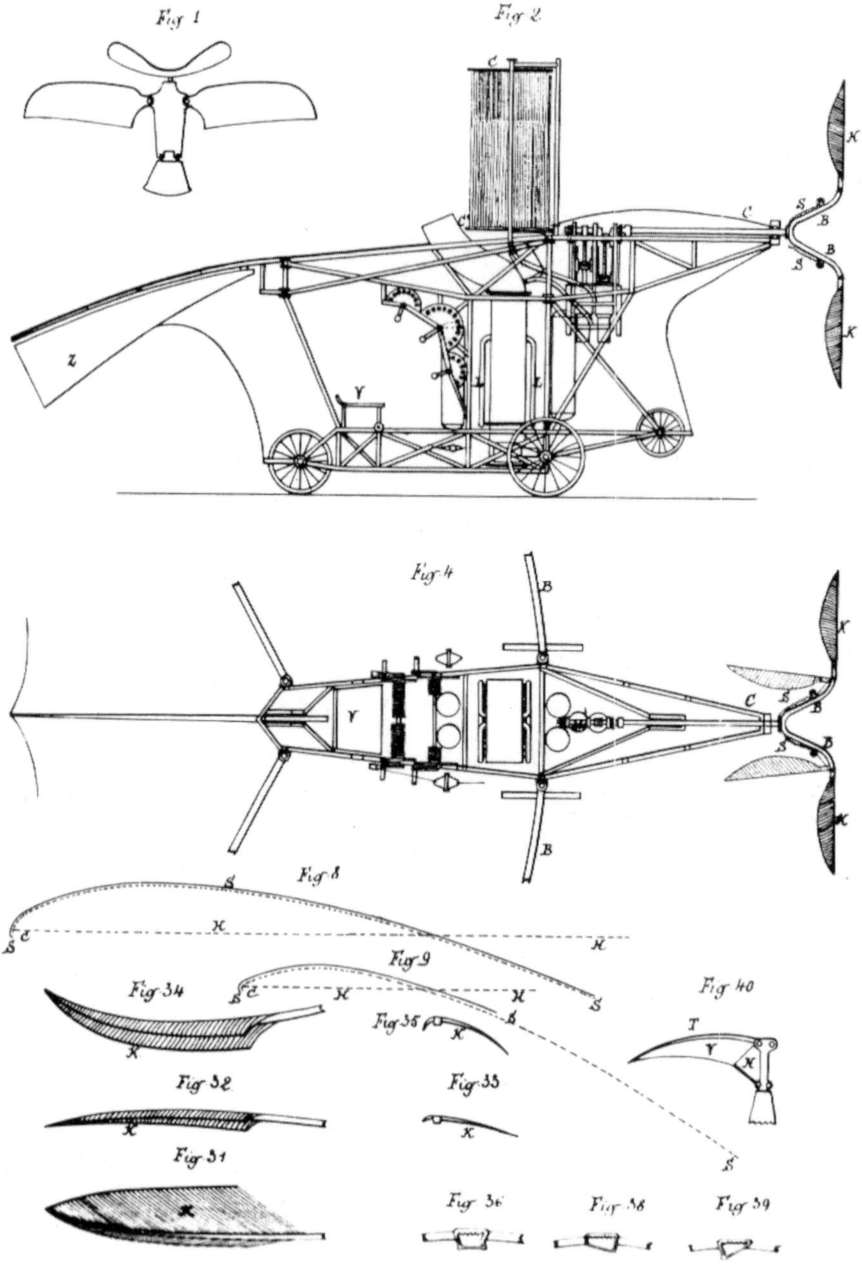

Figure 53. Line drawings of the *Éole* built by Clément Ader between 1882 and 1890.

The Aerostate de Poste

is extraordinary device was an eighteenth century French fantasy depicting long-distance aerial travel the twenty-fifth century. The caption which accompanied the original illustration went as follows: '*The rostate de Poste* which will leave on 10 March 2440 for China and countries *en route* to take postal :kets for Japan and smaller items for the island of Formosa (Taiwan). The price of the trip is 30 louis or louis if seated at the captain's table. All packets and parcels to be onboard by 1st of the month, latest. ssengers amusement will be catered for by 'aerial musicians' who will be available for concerts and ls. Towns who wish to be serenaded by the Great Organ must pay 25 louis.' Using a scale alongside the ›tion, the dimensions of this steam/jet propelled balloon can be calculated as follows: length 540ft; ght 660ft; balloon diameter 330ft.

e key to the letters and numbers on the plate is:

steam jet for propulsion. 2: the viewing telescope. 3: the great organ. 4: the cannon.
the hospital tent. 6: the stores and pumphouses. AAA: the globe. B: a statue of a cockerel.
the navigation light. D: the promenade gallery. E: the gas valve. F: officers' accommodation.
the ship's hull. H: the rudder. I: the steerman's house. K: the church. L: the captain's quarters. M: the
in steam pipe. N: the sails. O: ratlines to the gallery. P: passenger accomodation.
the magazine. R: the observation cage. S: the gangway to the cage. T: ornamental 'ailerons'.
the entry cabin (lowered to the ground). X: the 'brig'. Y: the musicians' gallery. Z: auxillary balloon.

B. In the eighteenth century 1 louis d'or equalled 1 English golden guinea. Roughly the prices translat- as £1,200 for normal travel, £2,000 to be seated at the captain's table and £1,000 if a town wished to serenaded.

e original plate was engraved and executed by R. A. Dante.

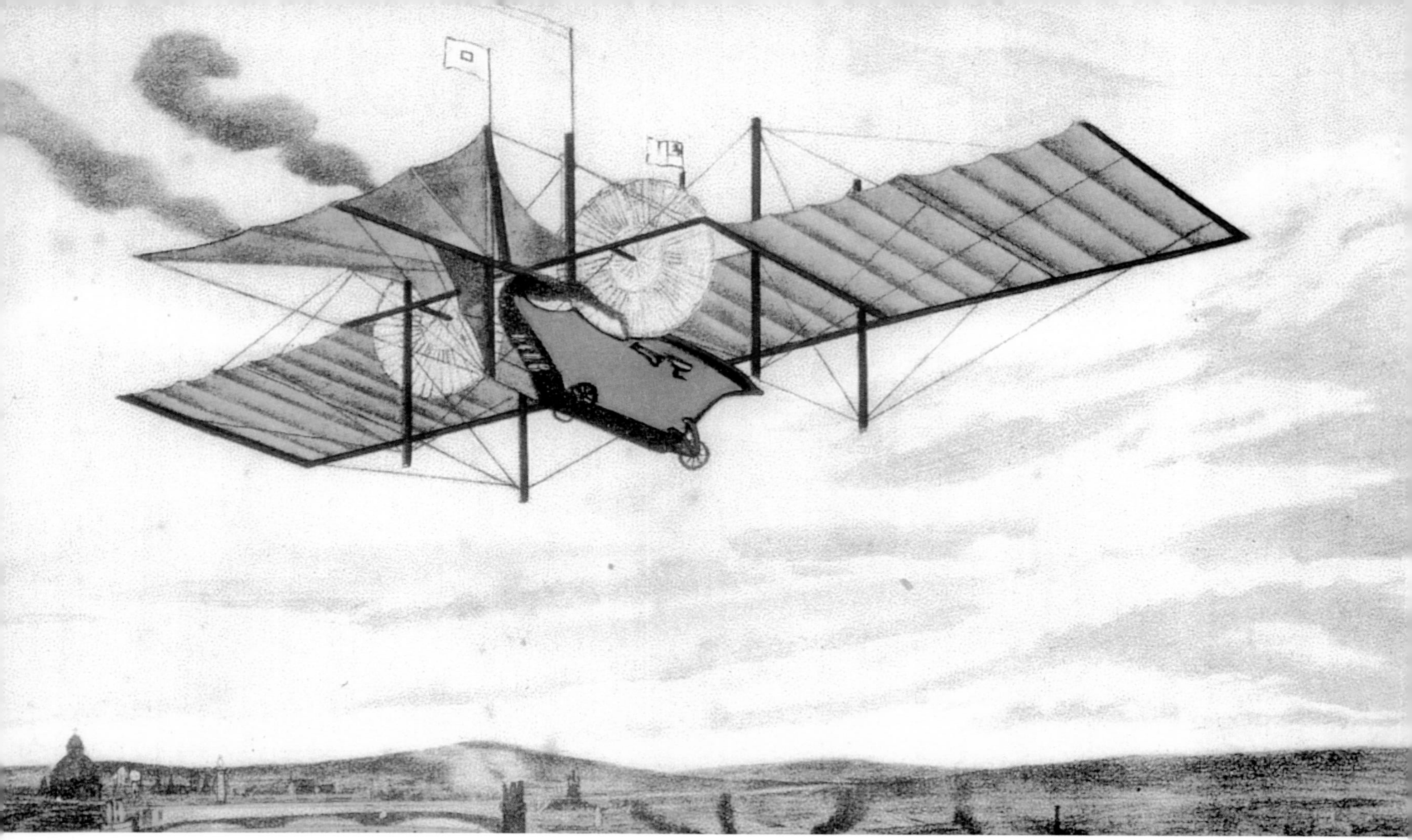

The *Aerial Steam Carriage* in flight over an industrial landscape

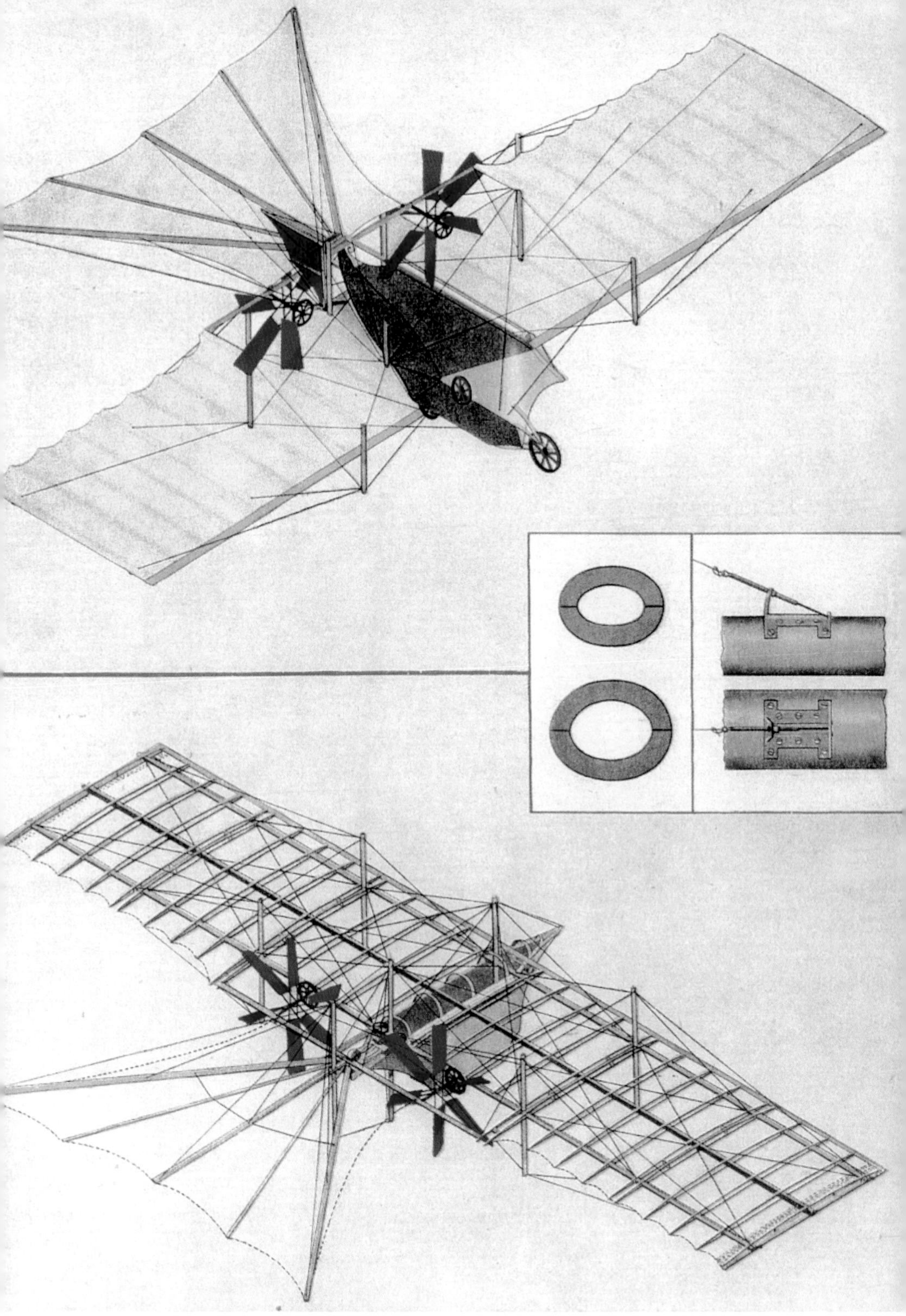

Top: Three-quarter view of the *Aerial Steam Carriage* from the underside.
Centre: Kingposts and method of rigging attachments.
Bottom: Skeletal view.

Henry Giffard's airship.

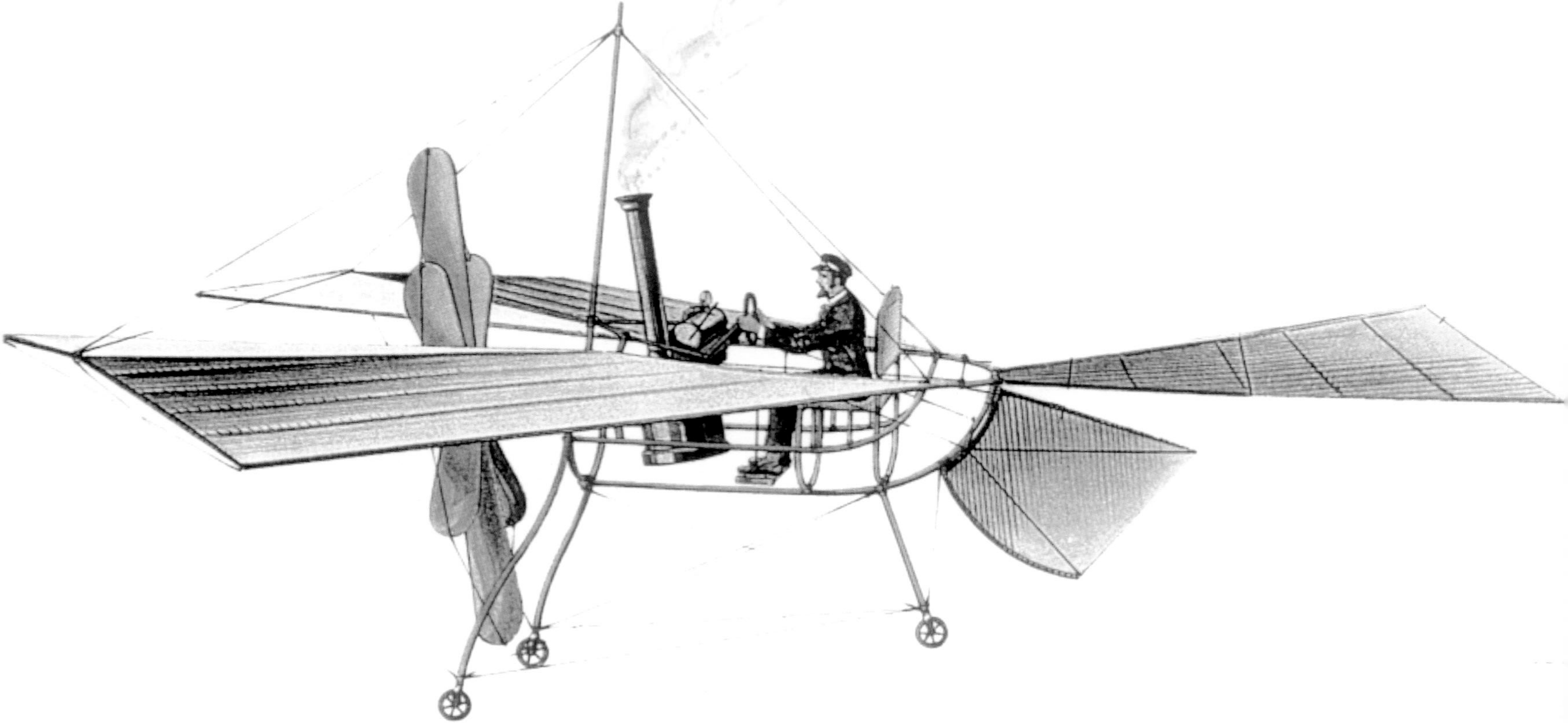

A conjectural illustration of the full-size monoplane constructed by Felix du Temple.

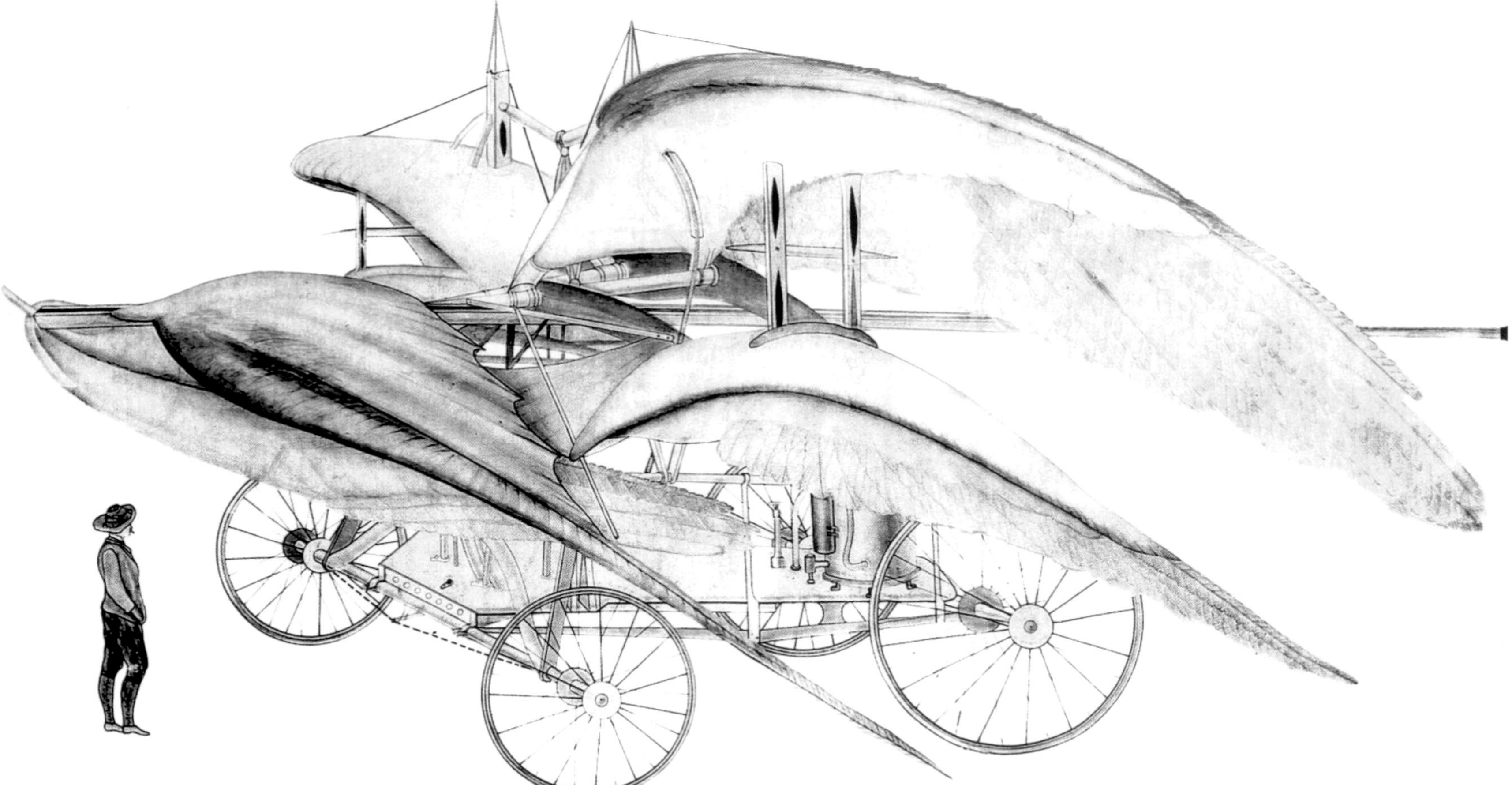

Edward Frost's Ornithopter of 1877.

A.F. Mozhaisskii's monoplane about to take off down an inclined wooden ramp.

The twin-engined version of the RUTAN aircraft.

Ronald Whitehouse demonstrating the OPUS power unit from the cockpit of a RUTAN aeroplane.

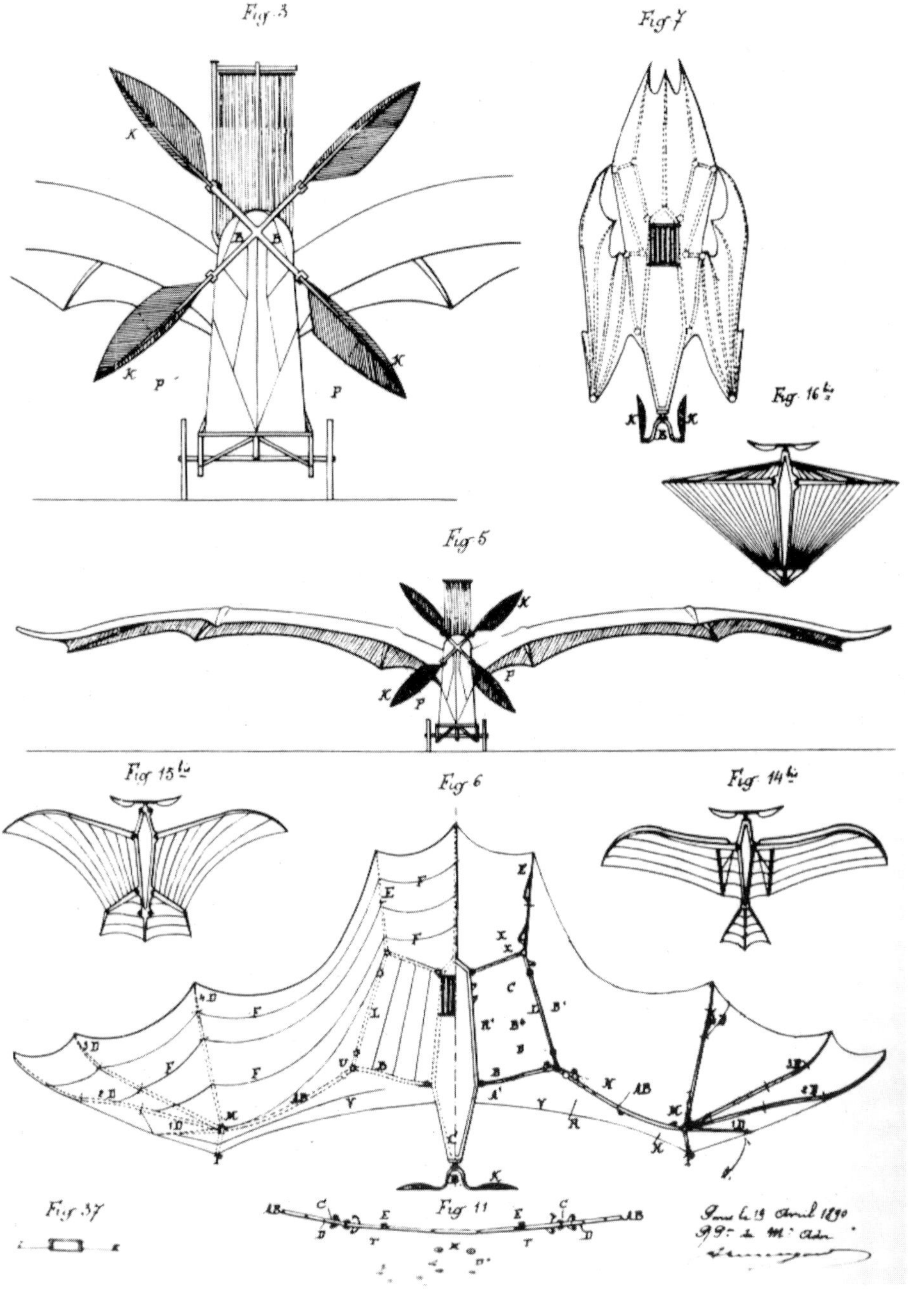
Fig 3
Fig 7
Fig 16 bis
Fig 5
Fig 15 bis
Fig 6
Fig 14 bis
Fig 37
Fig 11

for its rated power output. It was probably very similar in detail to those fitted to a later aircraft, the *Avion III*. In the *Éole*, the engine was mounted vertically in the inverted position and the crank-shaft drove the propeller via an extension. The boiler, which was of the tubular pattern, was mounted amidships, and an external condenser was fitted in a prominent location above the fuselage. The airscrew had four blades and it was made in the image of 'bird feathers'. The aeroplane rested on the ground on a three-wheeled undercart and had another wheel at the nose end to prevent it up-ending if it landed in an excessive nose-down attitude. Ader had originally envisaged using small crawler tracks in place of the wheels and in a popular illustration of the time (in *L'Illustration*), these were mistaken for skids (see fig. 52); the machine as tested at Armainvilliers ran on wheels. The cockpit position was at the rear, behind the boiler, and the pilot could not see forwards, only sideways out of two small windows. This inhibited him both when manoeuvring and when in flight, for his visibility was severely impaired. Ader claimed in 1906 that he had made a successful

Table 2. *Aircraft built by Clément Ader.*

	The *Éole*	The *Avion III*
Type	Single-engine tractor monoplane	Twin-engine tractor monoplane
Engine:	20 hp compound, steam	2 × 20 hp compound, steam
Bores	2.4 and 3.7 in	2.56 × 3.9 in
Stroke	3.9 in	3.9 in
Hp	–	20 @ 600 rpm
Boiler:	Multi-tubular	Multi-tubular
Pressure	–	140 psi
Outlet temp.	–	215° C
Hp rating	20	40
Condenser	Fuselage mounted, tubular	Fuselage mounted, tubular
Weight of engine	–	46 lb
Total weight of power unit	112 lb	258 lb
Airscrew	1 × feather type, bamboo	2 × feather type, bamboo
Diameters	6 ft 7 in	9 ft 10 in
Wingspan	45 ft 11 in	52 ft 6 in
Wing area	301.3 sq. ft	602.6 sq. ft
Length overall	21 ft 4 in	–
Weights:		
Airframe	387 lb	–
Plane empty	499 lb	569 lb
All-up, including pilot	653 lb	882 lb
Wing loading (approx.)	1.6 lb/sq. ft	2 lb/sq. ft

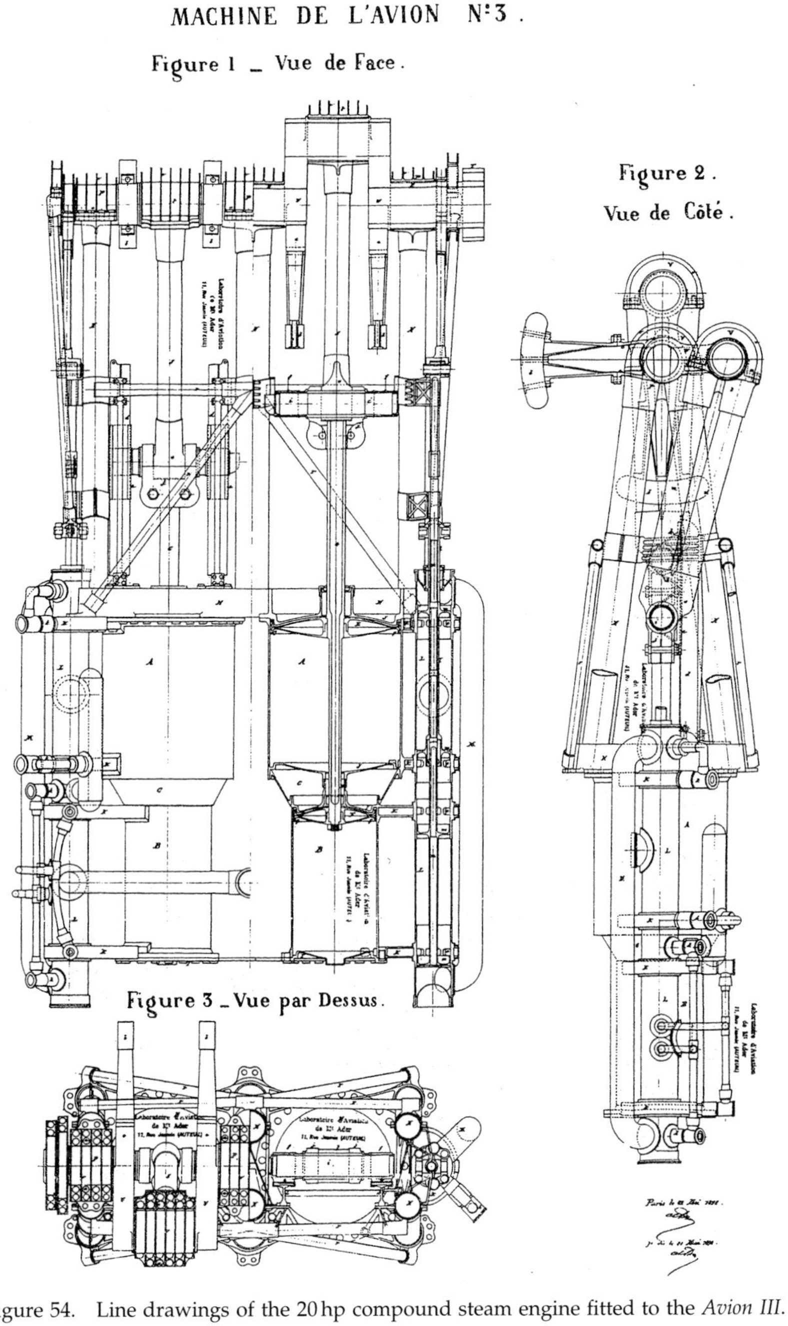

Figure 54. Line drawings of the 20 hp compound steam engine fitted to the *Avion III*.

flight at Satory with the *Éole* in September 1891 and that it had gone a distance of 100 metres, a claim that has never been verified and is certainly spurious.

Following his experiments with the *Éole*, Ader embarked upon the construction of another machine in 1892, named *Avion II*, but this was never completed. After abandoning it the building of the *Avion III* commenced, and was finished in 1897. It had similar wings to the *Éole*, but had a simplified control system which eliminated all wing movements except the 'swing-wing' element which was operated by means of a hand-crank needing some twenty to thirty turns to show any appreciable movement. The pilot, still installed in the rear cockpit behind the boiler but now out in the open, had a small vertical rudder controlled by two foot pedals, and a differential speed device for the two airscrews. The undercart consisted of a three-wheeled carriage and no nose wheel; these wheels were very small and the rear one was steerable and linked to the rudder. Originally the front wheels were fixed but later on they were fitted with a castor action system. Two of Ader's 20 hp compound steam engines were installed in the horizontal plane and their crankshafts drove twin contra-rotating, feather-style

Figure 54a. Ader's *Avion III* on view at the Salon Aeronautique in Paris.

airscrews whose arcs overlapped; the starboard or forward screw overlapped the port one by half its diameter. The blades of these airscrews were made from bamboo and designed to be flexible so that they adopted a finer pitch when the engines achieved maximum rpm in order to assist take-off. The multi-tubular boiler was fired by alcohol and, as in the *Éole*, was surmounted by an external condenser.

Ader claimed to have flown the *Avion III* at Satory, running around a circular track in 1897, before representatives of the French government and senior army officers. However, the 'flight' has been proven to be an invention and details of it have been discussed at length in another place, not being the concern of the present work.

The fate of the *Éole* is not known, and it has been assumed that the *Avion II*, which was not completed, became the basis for the *Avion III*. However, the latter aeroplane has been preserved at the Conservatoire des Arts et Métiers (Musée National des Techniques-CNAM), Paris, together with its engine.

Ader was subsidised by the French war ministry for work on the *Avion III* to the tune of 650,000 francs in 1892.

Hofmann

This German inventor made two experimental aircraft at the turn of the twentieth century, both of them were models, and flight was claimed for one. His machine used the force of gravity to become airborne in a novel manner. Usually gravitational force was used by means of a sloping ramp to achieve take-off but in the case of the Hofmann machine the necessary kinetic energy was generated by the use of collapsing legs or stilts which were attached to the body, or fuselage, of the aircraft. Prior to take-off the machine stood on the legs with its wings folded; at the point of take-off, the wings were unfolded and the engine started, and when sufficient propeller speed was attained the legs would suddenly be collapsed. The aircraft would instantly be aloft and ready to travel forwards. The idea behind this scheme was that with the aeroplane in mid-air, with its wings spread and its engine turning, it would then shoot off in flying mode!

The first model (see fig. 55) used a carbonic acid gas power plant, but the later version was driven by steam. This second model was built to a scale of 1/10 of full size and it was alleged to have flown in a large hall during a public demonstration. Hofmann may have been assisted by Mr P.Y. Alexander a well-known protagonist of flight at the time who had inherited some of the Henson and Stringfellow artifacts which he later donated to the Science Museum.

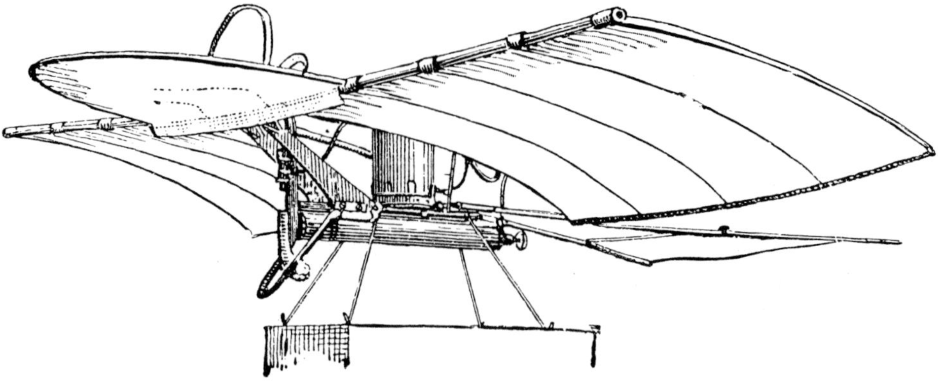

Figure 55. Hofmann's first machine which used a carbonic acid gas motor.

Figure 56. Hofmann's second steam-propelled aircraft.

Samuel Pierpoint Langley

This American pioneer had a lot of success with steam-driven model aircraft in the years just prior to the dawn of the twentieth century. He was an astronomer and scientist whose work, before he became interested in the technology of aviation, had included the exploration of the infra-red areas of the spectrum. He applied scientific principles to his work and used test equipment to investigate his theories; he used a 'whirling-wheel' which he built himself at Allegheny and which was capable of a peripheral speed of 70 mph. He was the First Secretary of the Smithsonian Institution in Washington DC, and he was a well respected savant. He had access to the institution's excellent workshop

Figure 57. Professor Samuel Pierpoint Langley.

and laboratory facilities and was therefore relieved from many of the problems that faced most of his contemporaries. He commenced his work in aeronautics in 1886 and at first used rubber power as a propellant, making a number of models with different configurations: biplanes, monoplanes and finally monoplanes with tandem wings. He concentrated on the development of the latter format, which had originally been conceived by D.S. Brown in 1873. All of this was done in the run-up to the construction of a full-sized aircraft in 1903.

Professor Langley always called his aircraft 'aerodromes' and throughout the ten years of experiment he stuck to the tandem-wing layout. After several minor problems he completed a large steam-powered model which he named the *Aerodrome No. 5* in 1896. He started testing this machine in the spring of that year, using a vessel moored on the Potomac River near Quantico, Virginia, just down river from Washington. This vessel, which has been variously described as a barge and a houseboat, was fitted with a catapult with which to launch his aeroplane into the air. The aeroplane had a wingspan of about 12 or 13 ft and its wings had elliptical tips; it was about 16 ft in length and was fitted with a steam engine, said to be a twin-cylinder unit of 1 hp; its boiler was fired by petroleum and the engine drove two propellers situated between the two sets of wings.

Early in May 1896 Langley set up the catapult on the boat some 20 ft above the surface of the river and projected his aeroplane into the air; the reason for performing the flight over water was to minimize any damage to the machine if it dropped. At the first attempt *Aerodrome No. 5*, launched against the wind, rose steadily into the air, gradually increasing its height until it reached an altitude of about 80–100 ft before the power unit ran out of steam and the craft glided down to alight safely on the waters. Altogether two recorded flights were made by this aircraft, possibly on 16 May 1896, and it seems that a distance of

Figure 58. Langley's *Aerodrome No. 5* taking off from the 'houseboat' moored on the Potomac River.

3,000 ft was achieved on the first and 4,200 ft on the second. These flights were the first sustained journeys made by a steam-driven aircraft; it was a pity that they were not controlled, but Langley never appeared to bother himself about the flight control of his model aircraft. These flights were witnessed by the great pioneer of telephony, Alexander Graham Bell who stated at the time: 'No one who witnesses the extraordinary spectacle of a steam engine flying with wings in the air, like a great soaring bird, could doubt for one moment the practicability of mechanical flight.' Another model was finished in 1896, and was named the *Aerodrome No. 6*. This model was tested, also on the Potomac River, on 28 November 1896. This machine was slightly different in that it had square wing tips and it is recorded that it was fitted with a 1¼ hp single-cylinder steam engine which worked at a pressure of 120 psi and produced 600 rpm at the airscrew. The cylinder had dimensions of 1.5 in bore by 2.75 in stroke and weighed in at 4.4 lb per hp (see figs. 59 and 60). It was also slightly larger than its predecessors, with a wingspan of some 14 ft; its flight in November lasted 45 seconds and covered a distance of 3,900 ft.

It seems that after these successes Langley lost interest in mechanical heavier-than-air flight and ended his experiments in 1898. However, with the onset of the Spanish-American War in the early years of the twentieth century, the US Government asked him to build a full-sized craft, and he collaborated with two other engineers, Charles M. Manly and Stephen M. Balzer. The latter built a precision rotary internal combustion engine for this craft, the first use of the rotary principle for aeronautical purposes. At the outset of the full-sized venture, Langley made a petrol driven version of his previous models to ¼ scale and this was flown successfully; it is thought to have been the first demonstration of an internal combustion engined aeroplane. However, when the full-sized plane was launched across the Potomac River on 7 October, with Manly on board, it crashed more or less immediately. In December, a second attempt was made, which also ended in failure, and the project was scrapped.

Figure 59. Representation of Langley's *Aerodrome No. 6* in flying attitude.

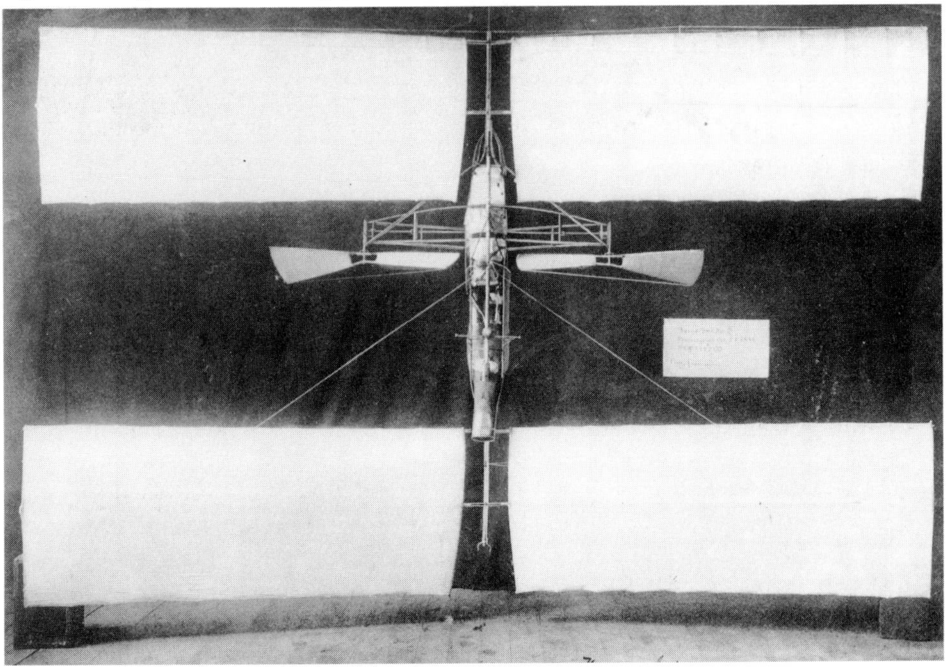

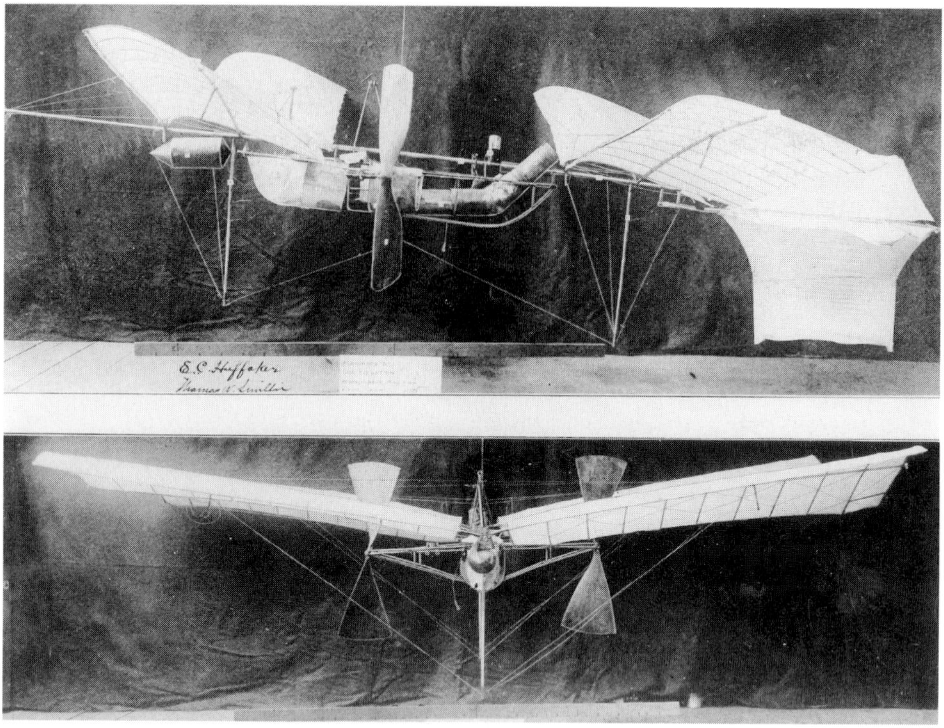

Figure 60. The arrangement of the wings, power unit and tailplane of the Langley steam-powered *Aerodrome No. 6.*

Sir Hiram Maxim

This expatriate American is famous for the invention of the Maxim quick-firing gun, for which he received his knighthood; he was also very interested in the science of mechanical, heavier-than-air flight, however, and he began experimenting in this field in 1887 when he was approached by a number of wealthy patrons, who asked him if he could build a flying machine. At the time Maxim estimated the cost of the undertaking as being in the region of £100,000 (an astronomical sum at that time, equating to about £2 million today), and that construction would take five years.

By 1889 he had formulated his ideas, which were published in the form of a patent, including details of the proposed aircraft and sketches of it (see figs. 61 and 61A). This specification (Brit. Pat. No. 16883 of 1889) showed a large plane surface from which hung a platform to support the power unit and the twin airscrews. Having indicated the direction in which he wished to proceed, Maxim employed two

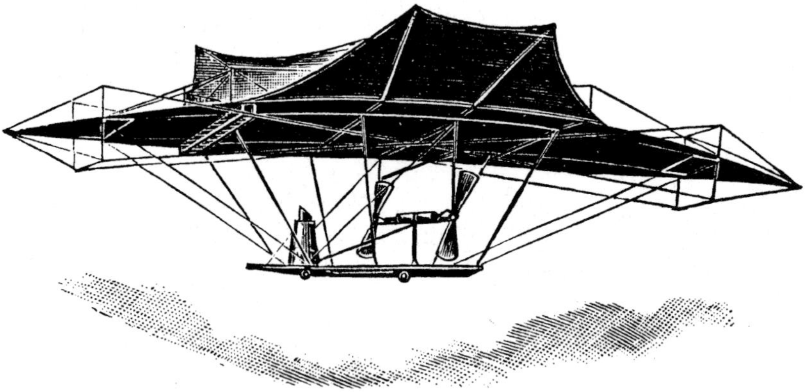

Figure 61. Sketch showing the arrangement of the Maxim aircraft.

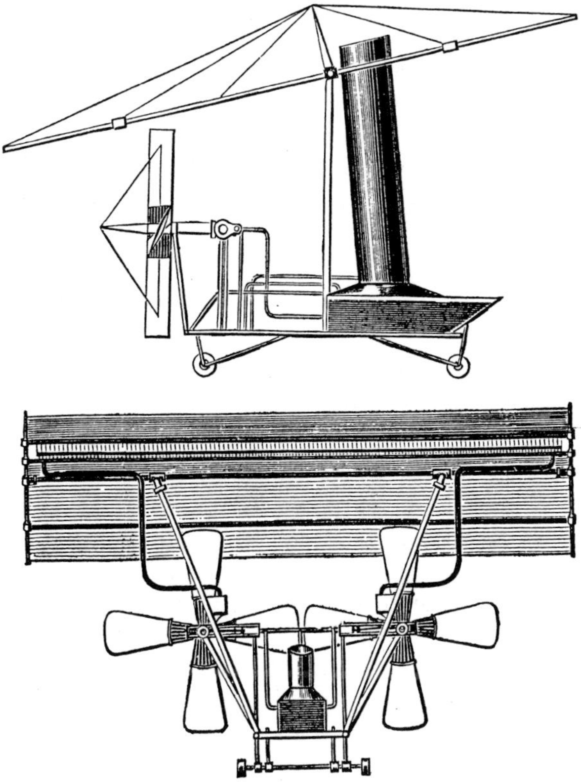

Figure 61A. Side and end elevation of the Maxim aircraft showing the disposition of the plane surface and the power unit and airscrews.

American mechanics to assist him with his work and he commenced operations at Baldwyns Park, near Bexleyheath in Kent. He chose steam power as his prime mover, for he said that after examining the Otto and Brayton internal combustion engines, he deduced that both were not developed enough and he declined to use them. He also said however: 'If small internal combustion engines could be had off the shelf I would not have bothered with steam at all.' This is odd, for Maxim had at least two US patents to his name for internal combustion engines! Another curious factor was his lack of basic knowledge of the construction and use of flying machines. He intimated that there was a misunderstanding regarding 'the action of aeroplanes' (meaning plane surfaces, not complete machines), and 'screws working in the air'. This was nonsense, for although Maxim had claimed that he had procured all the necessary literature on the subject, both in French and in English, he had obviously not studied the work of Cayley, Henson, Penaud, Tatin and others in depth. All along he was a 'groundsman' who never, ever, wished to go aloft.

Work on the Maxim creation commenced with the construction of an engine and boiler, together with experimentation into the operation and performance of airscrews; with the latter he eventually reduced

Figure 62. The main plane of the Maxim machine at Baldwyns Park.

the number of experimental propellers to eight units, and he invented an apparatus to test and measure thrust. This test rig consisted of a shaft mounted on two bearings with the screw affixed at one end, whilst at the other there was a strong spring connected to a pointer which registered the thrust in pounds on a segment of a circular dial that was graduated from 0 to 20. He also had another rig where the airscrew worked within a frame to which were attached a number of silken threads to denote the direction of air currents.

The first full-sized airscrew he made had a pitch of 24 ft, but this had too much drag, and the pitch was gradually reduced by experiment to 16 ft, then 14 ft and 12 ft, but none of them operated very well. The airscrews were made from a number of materials and these included American white pine and welded steel; he devised a special light-weight hub and tested all in a wind tunnel constructed to calibrate the efficiency of the propellers in airflow. Other experiments were conducted with aerofoil sections for both planes and airscrews over a period of time, as well as trying to build an efficient condenser which not only condensed steam, but also provided lift as well (figs. 61A, 62 and 63 show some of these items).

Figure 63. Maxim's aircraft at rest at Baldwyns Park.

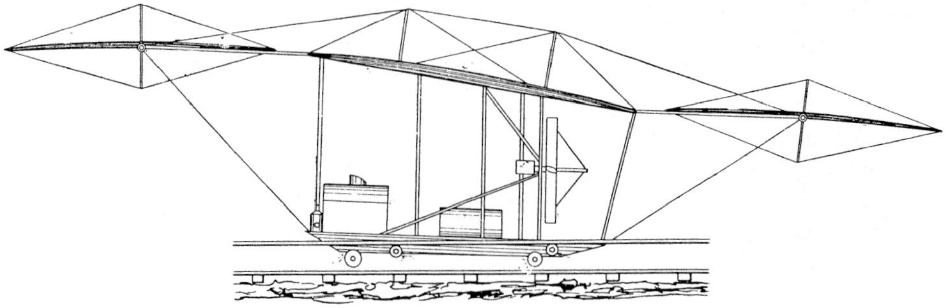

Figure 64A. Line drawing showing the disposition of the various plane surfaces in relation to the carriage work of the Maxim machine.

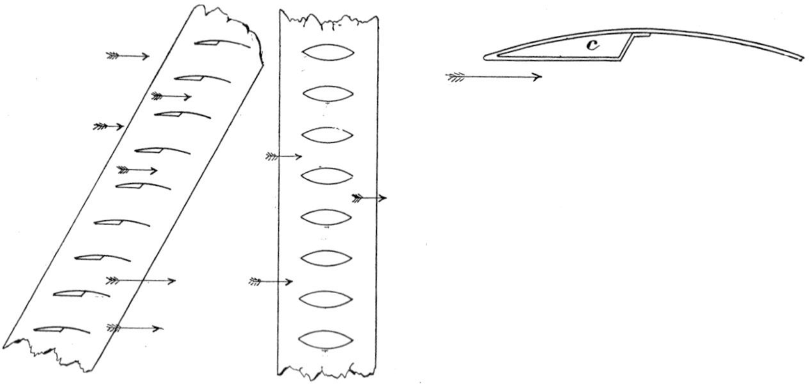

Figure 64B. Aerofoil sections used as a condenser on the Maxim machine.

Following this work and the trials associated with it, Maxim then went on to erect a rotating test rig on the basis laid down by Langley with his 'whirling table'; such rigs are still used today in space technology, and therefore, both Langley and Maxim were well ahead of their time. This apparatus was used for showing the effectiveness of aerofoils etc.; it was driven by a steam engine which also drove a tachometer and a dynamometer. At the same time the effectiveness of tractor and pusher airscrews were compared.

Sir Hiram Maxim seemed to have conducted his experiments in an exemplary scientific manner, but somewhere the results appeared to be flawed, perhaps because he was something of a showman. From the research using the 'whirling table' with planes rotating in a circle 200 ft in circumference, he went on to attempt to 'fly' them in a straight line to obviate the problem of them already entering disturbed air; these

Figure 65. Model of Sir Hiram Maxim's flying machine.

Figure 66. View showing airscrews and power unit installation in the Maxim machine.

tests were conducted at the Crystal Palace. Later he built a 'captive flying machine' which he demonstrated at Thurlow Park. This apparatus consisted of a boat fitted with aerofoil planes and driven along by an electric motor; he even discussed the idea of using it as a fairground attraction in order to finance more experiments! Experiments were also made during this time with gyroscopes to compensate for pitching and yawing. Eventually a model of the proposed flying machine was made. Also an experimental plane which was, in effect an elevator (see fig. 67), using a framework of steel with the fore and aft edges of tightly drawn wires covered with silk or balloon fabric was made. This plane was 50 ft wide and had an area of 1,500 sq. ft. Other major components were completed, until the whole machine was assembled.

Maxim's aeroplane was a huge contrivance with a wingspan of 104 ft, a wing area of 4,000 sq. ft and an all-up weight of 8,000 lb. It was a biplane with an enormous centre surface and four outrigger planes together with fore and aft elevators; it had no rudder. Two large airscrews of 17 ft 10 in in diameter were driven by a pair of compound steam engines, each one producing 180 hp. It was definitely the largest steam-powered aircraft to have been made and it would have flown if Maxim had not designed a special outrigger wheel and railway track to

Figure 67. One of the elevators for the Maxim machine.

restrain it. However, it would have most certainly crashed, as its control system was not conducive to providing sustained flight.

When the time came to run the machine, a railway track was laid at Baldwyns Park made from steel rails to a gauge of 9 ft, each side of which was a safety track made 2 ft higher at a width of 30 ft. The idea of the safety track was to inhibit the lift of the aircraft if it actually flew. An accident occurred when one of the outrigger wheels fitted to restrain the machine from flying gave way, allowing the rear end of the aeroplane to go free; this in turn placed strain upon other parts of the structure of the restraining mechanism, and the whole machine ran out of control. Control was regained, however, by the simple expedient of shutting off the steam. Unfortunately the right forward outrigger wheel had torn up 100 ft of the 3 in × 9 in Georgia pine wooden safety track, whereupon the craft sank back to earth to embed itself into the soft grass. One of the pine timbers went through the fabric of one of the lower planes and shredded it, and one of the airscrews was also badly damaged. This accident was probably caused by premature lift, which caught the crew of four men off guard. Unfortunately, the mishap spelled the end of Sir Hiram's work for it appears that he had also run out of money. Although he had estimated the cost of the work to be about £100,000 it was reported that the actual sum expended was only £20,000 – still a very large amount of money at that time.

Table 3. *The Power Units for Sir Hiram Maxim's Steam Aircraft.*

Type of engine	Horizontal, compound steam engine – 2 off
No. of cylinders	2 each
Area hp piston	20 sq. in
Area lp piston	50.26 sq. in
Stroke	12 in
Max. hp	180 each – total rated hp 360
Hp steam	320 psi @ cut-off ¾ stroke
Lp steam	125 psi @ cut-off ⅝ stroke
Power lost in airscrew slip	150 hp
Power driving ancillaries	80.3 hp
Power actually used in lifting aircraft	133.33 hp
Total power output	363.63 hp (N.B. These engines running together with a hp steam alone could achieve a figure of 500 hp to present a power to weight ratio of 1 bhp per lb.)
Total weight of each engine	320 lb

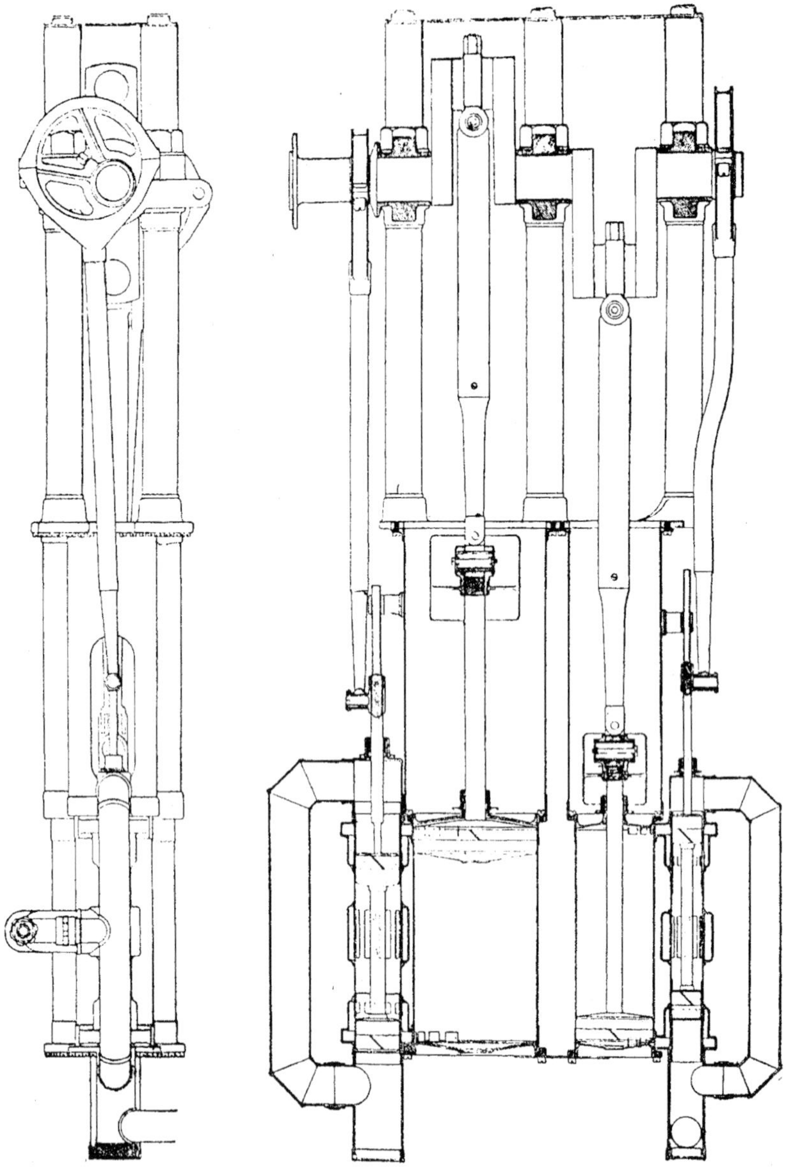

I.—HORIZONTAL SECTION AND SIDE ELEVATION OF THE ENGINE.

Nearly every part of these engines is constructed of tubular steel. Piston-valves are employed, and all the moving parts are of tempered steel and exceedingly light.

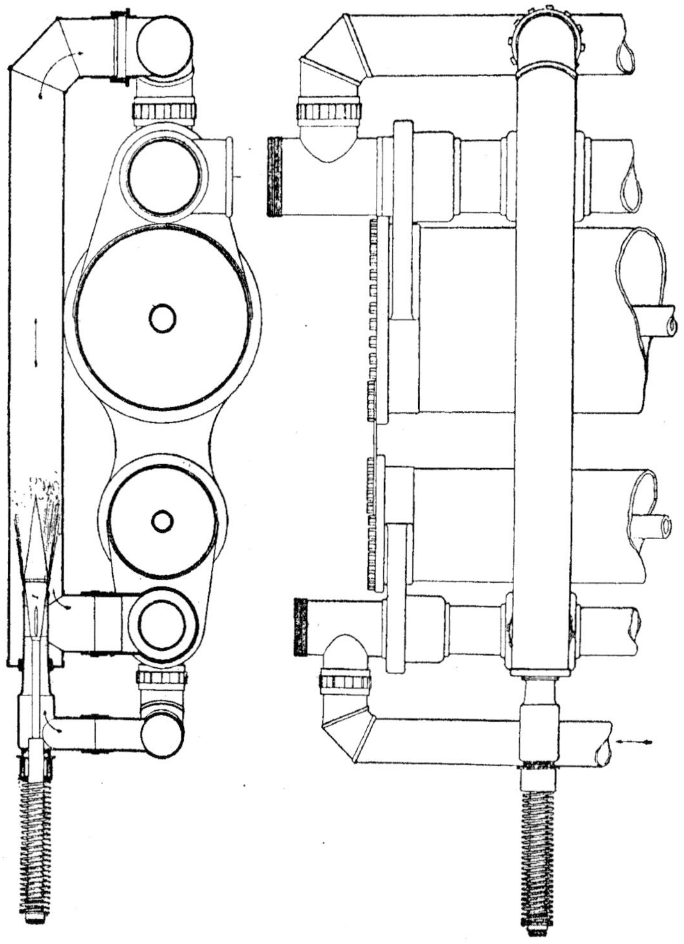

2.—PLAN OF TRANSVERSE SECTION OF THE ENGINE.

Showing the by-pass, which consists of a species of injector, and which allows steam to pass directly from the high-pressure supply to the low-pressure cylinder, producing more direct pressure on the low-pressure piston than back pressure in the high-pressure cylinder. This valve may be adjusted so that if the pressure should rise above a certain point, instead of blowing off at the safety-valve, it blows past the high-pressure cylinder in the manner shown.

Figure 68. One of the 180 hp compound steam engines used to power Sir Hiram Maxim's huge craft.

Figure 69. The massive tubular boiler of the craft.

Figure 69a. Sir Hiram Maxim demonstrates the lightness of his power unit.

Figure 70. The multiple jet burner element.

The engineering of the Maxim machine was excellent, for the powerful engines could accelerate this huge equipage to a speed of 42 mph, after which it was proved that it had the ability to lift off. The *pièce de résistance* of the whole design was the power unit. At first a Herreshoff type of boiler was fitted, but for some reason this was thought to be unsuitable and Maxim decided to design and construct his own generator. He produced the special unit, which is shown in fig. 69. This was a large affair, as can be seen by the figure of the assistant standing alongside it. It was 8 ft long, 4 ft 6 in wide and 6 ft high, and with its casing and dome weighed just under 1,000 lb. It was of the multiple water tube style, using special thin tubing that had been imported from France. It was tested to a pressure of 400 psi and it worked at a maximum pressure of 320 psi. A special gas burner was fitted with a matrix of 7,650 jets to provide a continuous flame along the whole of the boiler (see fig. 70).

There is no doubt that Maxim's achievement was great but it was costly, it did not apparently achieve much in the way of added knowledge and the design and plan had scientific flaws. His other flight patent was Brit. Pat. No. 19228 of 1891.

Gustave Whitehead

This pioneer, who is known to have constructed some aircraft between 1899 and 1902 was an enigmatic personality whose claims have never really been officially substantiated. His image was not as prominent as, say, Sir Hiram Maxim or Professor Langley, but nevertheless he does have a place in the history of aviation despite the adverse remarks that have been made concerning his efforts; he was one of the protagonists of the use of steam propulsion for powered flights.

He was born on New Year's Day in 1874 in Bavaria with the surname of Weisskopf which was later anglicized when he went to the USA in

1895. Whilst living in Germany he constructed a crude glider at the age of thirteen which he attempted to fly by jumping off the roof of his parents' house: it would appear that this 'flight' was unsuccessful but it did imbue within him the spirit of aviation which stayed with him. Later on he is said to have worked on gliders with that famous exponent of flight, Otto Lilienthal, in his homeland, but on the death of his parents during his teens he left Germany for Brazil. He was only in South America for a short time before he sought employment at sea; he pursued this career for about six years before going to the USA. He settled in Boston and then moved to Buffalo, NY. He busied himself with the problems of heavier-than-air flight whilst working in a carriage works at Tenawanda. By 1899 he was living in Pittsburgh and working as a part-time employee in a coal mine.

The Whitehead family lived in premises on Bates Street, Pittsburgh, and it was here that Gustave began to build aircraft seriously. As a source of power for his aeroplane he experimented with steam, and he strove to perfect a lightweight pressure vessel. These experiments were alarming and eventually alienated his neighbours, who were increasingly irritated by Whitehead's antics, which were dangerous in the extreme! His idea was to use thinner and thinner gauges of sheet metal of various types until he arrived at the minimum thickness which would sustain the pressure needed to power his engine. He made a series of boilers which he tested to destruction whilst recording the pressure attained during each attempt. These experiments, usually conducted at night, created loud explosions and sometimes broke windows in the neighbourhood, so Whitehead was soon a pariah in the area. Presumably he found a satisfactory solution to the boiler problem for, in

Figure 71. The duplex unidirectional and double-acting power unit as used in the 1899 'flight'.

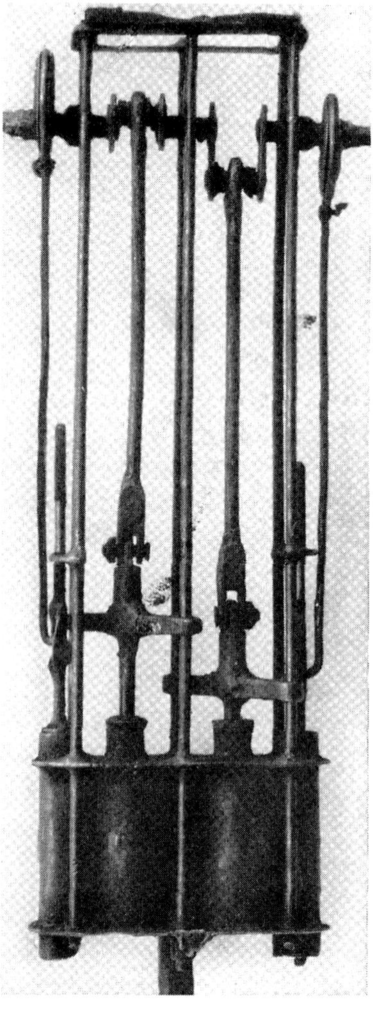

1899, he built a full-sized aeroplane which was powered by a twin-cylinder duplex, steam engine (see fig. 71). It is believed that he did some tests on the airframe as a glider which bore some similarity to the work of Lilienthal, before making a powered attempt in order to prove its airworthiness. The success of these trials has never been documented.

Whitehead's claims to effective powered flight were supported by a number of witnesses, who signed affidavits to the effect that they saw his machine take off in Schenley Park or nearby in Pittsburgh in the spring of 1899; these affidavits were taken over thirty years after the event, however, and lapses of memory must be taken into account. However, in 1945, Orville Wright writing in the magazine *US Air Services* threw a different light upon the story, for he referred to the 'myth of Gustave Whitehead having made a powered flight in 1901'. This second flight was alleged to have taken place at Bridgeport, Connecticut on 14 August and Wright claimed that it was nothing but a publicity stunt on the part of the local newspaper, the *Bridgeport Herald* which ran it to discredit the successful work of others.

Returning to the 1899 event, the most important of the affidavits was signed by Louis Darvarich on 19 July 1934 but it does not reveal the exact date that the flight was supposed to have been made; there has also been no recorded evidence to substantiate a date in 1899 in other published work. Davarich stated in his evidence:

> *In approximately April or May 1899, I was present and flew with Mr Whitehead on the occasion when he succeeded in flying his machine, propelled by steam motor, on a flight of approximately a half-mile distance at a height of about 20 to 25ft from the ground. This flight occurred in Pittsburgh, and the type of machine used by Mr Whitehead was a monoplane. We were unable to rise high enough to avoid a three-storey building in our path and when the machine fell I was scalded severely by the steam for I have been firing the boiler. I was obliged to spend several weeks in hospital and I recall the incident of the flight very clearly. Mr Whitehead was not injured, as he had been in the front part of the machine, steering it.*

The accident referred to has never been proved by any hospital records; the two hospitals nearest to the scene of the flight were the Mercy Hospital and the Western Pennsylvania Hospital and they both denied any knowledge of the admission of a patient by the name of Davarich during the period in question. The Nursing Superintendent of the former hospital wrote in a letter dated 4 September 1934 that despite a detailed search of the records for 1899, no person in the name of Davarich had been admitted; on the same date a letter from the other hospital also confirmed that they had no record of such an admission. Other hospitals in the Pittsburgh area also denied any knowledge of the admission of a patient by that name in 1899. However, Davarich did not speak English and after a lapse of thirty-five years there could have been a problem with the original records; moreover such records could have been destroyed by 1934.

Charles L. Richey of Pittsburgh also signed an affidavit on 21 August 1936, stating:

I recall that around the year 1900 I saw and talked to a man by the name of Whitehead (or a similar name) as he demonstrated an airplane in Schenley Park, Pittsburgh, Pennsylvania, which he was supposed to have made. I also saw him run the engine for some time using charcoal as a fuel. I did not see the plane in flight as it was anchored to the ground at the time I saw it. I do recall reading about and hearing of this plane making a flight in which it was supposed to have gained a height of about 20 ft and then it crashed, injuring the driver. I readily recognized pictures shown to me by Miss Stella Randolph as being much like the plane, and the photograph she showed me very much resembled the man who was in charge of the plane I saw in Schenley Park.

Another witness, Martin Devine of Pittsburgh, a fireman at No. 24 Engine House in the city, gave a statement on oath on 15 August 1936, which ran as follows:

I recall the late Gustave Whitehead and an airplane of his construction which I helped to push, upon more than one occasion, for a demonstration. The plane was heavy, and I do not recall being present on the occasion of its flight, but I believe I arrived immediately after it crashed into a newly built brick building, a newly constructed apartment house which, I believe, was on the O'Neal Estate. I recall that someone was hurt and taken to a hospital, but I do not recall what one. I am able to identify the inventor as Gustave Whitehead from the picture of this man showed me by Miss Stella Randolph. The plane was heated by charcoal and the place of most of the experiments was in the vicinity of the present McKee Place and Louisa Avenue .... As definitely as I can recall the plane was upon wheels.

Yet another witness, John A. Johns, has also recalled seeing the Whitehead machine in the location mentioned by Martin Devine but someone else, William Burns, whose father was a fireman at the No. 24 Engine House at the time said that the event took place opposite the fire station at the corner of Wilmot and Ward Streets. So there appears to be some conflict concerning the exact location of the flight, although all of them are close; however, the location given by Davarich was opposite No. 24 Engine House.

Gustave Whitehead's 1899 flight is as contentious as that of Clément Ader but as there were supporting witnesses it is possible that his aircraft did get off the ground; it is unlikely , however, that sustained flight was achieved and so the validity of the Wright Brothers' achievement is unaffected. The 1901 attempt, which was reported in the *Bridgeport Herald*, followed the move of Whitehead and Davarich first to New York City and then to Bridgeport, Connecticut, where the pair constructed another aeroplane. The newspaper article, which was published on 18 August stated:

> *Mr Whitehead, last Tuesday night, with two assistants, took his machine to a long field back of Fairfield, and the inventor for the first time flew his machine for half-a-mile. It worked perfectly, and the operator found no difficulty in handling it. Mr. Whitehead's machine is equipped with two engines, one to propel it on the ground, on wheels, and the other to make the wings or propellers work. In order to fly, the machine is speeded to a sufficient momentum on the ground by the lower engine and then the engine running the propellers is started which raises the machine in the air at an angle of about six degrees. The engine in this flight is reported to be a petrol motor.*

The flight was said to have been made on property owned by the Bridgeport Gas Company.

This story did not emerge until the weekend after the alleged flight, and it is strange that such an earth-shattering event was held back for four days despite being witnessed by the *Herald* reporter Howell. Moreover, there was an element of facetiousness in the article, for it was entitled 'Flying' and was illustrated with four witches flying on broomsticks!

The 1901 report said that four people were present on the occasion of the Bridgeport flight: Gustave Whitehead, Andrew Cellie and James Dickie plus the reporter from the newspaper. James Dickie said in an affidavit dated 2 April 1937 that he had worked with Whitehead on aeroplane construction but was unable to corroborate the press article; his evidence went as follows:

> *I do not know Andrew Cellie, the other man who is supposed to have witnessed the flight of August 14, 1901, described in the* Bridgeport Herald. *I believe the entire story in the* Herald *was imaginary, and grew out of the comments of Whitehead in discussing what he hoped to get from his plane. I was not present and did not witness any airplane flight on*

August 14, 1901. I do not remember or recall ever hearing of a flight with this particular plane or any other that Whitehead ever built.

John J. Dvořák, a Chicago businessman who was eventually employed on the teaching staff of the Washington University of St Louis in 1904, said that he also worked with Whitehead at Bridgeport and financed the production of an engine suitable for aviation purposes. This was, presumably, the 'petrol motor' used in the alleged flight. Dvořák came to the conclusion that Whitehead was incapable of making a satisfactory power unit and withdrew from the arrangement; in an affidavit dated 18 July 1936 he stated:

I personally do not believe that Whitehead ever succeeded in making any airplane flights. Here are my reasons: (1) Whitehead was given to gross exaggeration, (2) Whitehead did not possess sufficient mechanical skill and equipment to build a successful motor. He was eccentric – a visionary and a dreamer to such an extent that he actually believed what he merely imagined. He had delusions.

Another gentleman, one Stanley Y. Beach, wrote an article in the *Scientific American* at the time of the 1901 'flight' which was illustrated with pictures of Whitehead's endeavours, and he said that the inventor had never told him that he had flown in one of his machines. Beach was associated with Whitehead from 1901 to 1910 and he had induced his father to finance further experiments to the tune of $10,000 but during that period he believed that none of the Whitehead aeroplanes ever left the ground.

Gustave Whitehead was a perfectionist and a visionary who was always dissatisfied with his efforts; he had studied bird flight, just as many of his predecessors and contemporaries had done, and when one of his experimental flights was completed he started rebuilding the machine immediately in order to create 'the perfect flying machine'. As with many inventors, his programme was one of constant experiment with total finality never achieved.

The airframe used in the 1901 machine had a body or fuselage 16 ft long, was ribbed with a light wooden framework over which was stretched canvas. It weighed about 50 lb. The wings were built of a framework of mild steel and bamboo and the wingspan was 35 ft; a covering of 450 sq. ft of white silk provided the lifting surface. The rudder, measuring 10 ft in length was made in a similar fashion to the wings; a mast or kingpost as well as a 'bowsprit' gave additional strength to both wings and tail. This construction can be seen clearly in figs. 72 and 73, for all Whitehead's airframes were of a similar design.

Figure 72. A recent construction of Whitehead's machine.

The whole of the Whitehead saga appears to be shrouded in mystery but one thing is certain: he was a true pioneer who built heavier-than-air machines that were loosely based upon the work of Otto Lilienthal. His first aircraft was driven by steam and there is a possibility that one of them became airborne for a short period of time. Later flights in the early years of the twentieth century appear to be pure fabrication and a

Figure 73. Whitehead with the first of his aeroplanes and its steam engine.

latter claim that Whitehead flew for a distance of 7 miles over Long Island Sound seems to be patently absurd.

Frederick John Stringfellow (1832–1905)

It has often been said that history repeats itself, and so it was with the science of aerial steam navigation, for many enthusiasts and pioneers either ignored the work of their predecessors or were unaware of it, and therefore repeated what had gone before. However, F.J. Stringfellow, the son of John Stringfellow (see chapters 1 and 2), continued the work of his father after a lapse of some time, and he produced some interesting steam-powered aircraft during the final decades of the nineteenth century.

The Second Aeronautical Exhibition had been held in the Banqueting Hall at the Alexandra Palace in 1885. Soon afterwards, probably hearing of the work of F.J. Stringfellow, the Aeronautical Society offered him space to work on and test his machines. It has been reported that he started work in 1886, some three years after his father's death, but the writer believes that he did so much earlier, for some authorities indicate that the aeroplane he was working on was not quite completed and that he could not avail himself of the offer as he had to continue working as a dentist in order to make ends meet.

The fact remains that Stringfellow did follow in his father's footsteps, and that he used all the information amassed thus far to produce improved versions of the original aeroplanes of the 1840s. His initial machine was a biplane based on the premise of his father's original 1848 monoplane; he used a similar wing layout but reversed the positions of the airscrews to make the first tractor biplane aircraft. The fact that he was working along the correct lines is shown in fig. 74 which depicts a very modern design that would have been acceptable twenty years later. To power the aeroplane a very neat and well engineered engine and boiler unit was built, along the lines of his father's work.

In 1892, Stringfellow published a pamphlet entitled *A Few Remarks on What Has Been Done with Screw-Propelled Aero-Plane Machines from 1809 to 1892*, in which space was devoted to the biplane model. It stated that the wingspan of the top plane was 10 ft and that of the lower one 8 ft 10 in, to give a total wing area of 27 sq. ft; these wings had a rigid leading edge and a 'feathered' trailing edge. The airscrews were handed to give a contra-rotating effect and they were about 27 in in diameter. His remarkable engine was fitted with a cone and cylinder boiler with 16 cones 7½ in long and 1¼ in in diameter at their upper end. The cylindrical 'super-heating chamber' was 12 in long by 2½ in in diameter, with over 2 sq. ft of effective heating surface. It produced

Figure 74. The steam-powered biplane fitted with twin tractor airscrews constructed by F.J. Stringfellow.

steam at a pressure of 100 psi. A single-cylinder engine with a bore of 1.1875 completed this unit and it was capable of a rotational speed of 600 rpm. The whole ensemble weighed but 18½ lb in working order, including water and alcohol fuel. This aeroplane was reminiscent of the 1848 machine but with an extra set of wings added and the propellers fitted at the front.

Whether or not Stringfellow ever flew his aeroplanes has been debated over the years, but there are statements from at least two witnesses to say that he did. A Mrs F.S. Hann said in 1972 that she remembered seeing a flying machine built by a Mr Stringfellow of Chard flying over some fields near Crewkerne 'like a huge bird'. Another witness, a sexton, said that his father had told him that he had seen a flying machine aloft on Bincombe Hill. Stringfellow built at least two aircraft, the biplane already mentioned and a quintuplane version which was exhibited at the Aeronautical Exhibition of 1903, again at the Alexandra Palace – the only heavier-than-air, powered machine to be shown there. Which aeroplane the witnesses claimed to have seen is uncertain.

The quintuplane was similar to the biplane in that it had a power car like the ones used in the 1848 original and in the biplane, and it had the same form of tail unit as in those earlier aircraft. The wings were of decreasing span downwards and had filled-in interplane struts, five between each wing; these wings were of parallel chord with square wingtips. Stringfellow was also responsible for building four steam engine sets, some of which he may have sold on.

In his will of 1879, John Stringfellow had left the artifacts and models known as the 'Crystal Palace models' to his son whilst most of the other models went to trustees and remained in store for a very long time. It is also known that F.J. often suffered from lack of finance and sold some of his legacy to others to raise money. Most went to C.H.M. Alderson and P.Y. Alexander who, after Stringfellow's death allowed them to be saved for the National Collection, where they remain to this day.

Frederick Stringfellow was a serious exponent of powered flight and he knew, and was in correspondence with, many of the leading aeronauts of the day, including F.W. Breary, Thomas Moy, Horatio Phillips, and the President of the Aeronautical Society, Major B.F.S. Baden-Powell. He also knew, in detail, the work of Professor S. Langley, Sir Hiram Maxim, Octave Chanute and others and was, therefore, well versed in the science of aeronautics.

Chapter Four

The Twentieth Century

The twentieth century saw a waning of interest in the use of steam engines to propel aircraft as lighter and more compact power units were developed from 1900 onwards. The invention of the internal combustion engine which did not require an external source of energy made the realization of the heavier-than-air machine a probability rather than a mere possibility. It has already been noted that when a petrol engine was used in place of steam there was a marked increase in the power-to-weight availability, which achieved much better results. This was shown particularly in the Frost ornithopter, for when the steam engine, albeit of very small power, was used the machine did not move at all from the ground, but when an internal combustion engine was substituted in 1904 the machine managed to leap up and down at each wing stroke.

Nevertheless, experiments with steam during the course of the century provided some very interesting results. It was in the 1930s that a successful, sustained, manned and controlled heavier-than-air flight was made using a steam engine. It followed some very useful attempts with model aircraft in the years just before and just after the First World War. Other uses of steam power in aviation were mooted in the 1930s, with turbines specified to act as an auxiliary means of power in propulsion systems. Again, after the Second World War, when atomic power was being investigated for a number of peaceful uses, schemes were put forward for giant airships using steam turbine power plants, but they were either impractical or downright fanciful.

At the end of the nineteenth century, the people who had more or less got it right – the Stringfellows, du Temple, Tatin and others who had suggested lightweight machines with adequate control surfaces – had paved the way for the design of effective model aircraft as a precursor to the goal of sustained and controlled manned flight using steam engines. The work done by H.H. Groves in the early years of the twentieth century proved that this form of steam-powered flight with models was possible. There were others before Groves who used external combustion power, but not with the same degree of success.

Lawrence Hargrave

This Australian has already been mentioned in connection with compressed-air powered ornithopters (see chapter 2). Between 1896 and 1903 he progressed from experiments with flapping-winged aircraft to propeller-driven machines which had the ability to land and take off from water. The first of these was described in 1896 (see fig. 75) and was probably driven by compressed air. A later craft, believed to have been made in 1902 used a wing plan similar to that put forward by Horatio Phillips and, in model form, was made from tin-plate fitted with a small steam engine (see fig. 76).

Trajan Vuia (1872–1950)

This Paris-based Romanian built an interesting aircraft that was driven by an extraordinary form of external combustion derived in a way from steam technology. It was named the *Vuia No. 1* and it featured the use of a carbonic acid gas motor supplied by Léon Serpollet. It was a strange contraption which had a single bat-like wing built in the manner of those constructed by Otto Lilienthal; it rested on a four-wheeled undercarriage which supported a platform carrying the power unit and provided seating for the pilot. Vertical control surfaces were attached beneath the wing and the machine was probably the first

Figure 75. The propeller-driven floatplane proposed by Lawrence Hargrave in 1896.

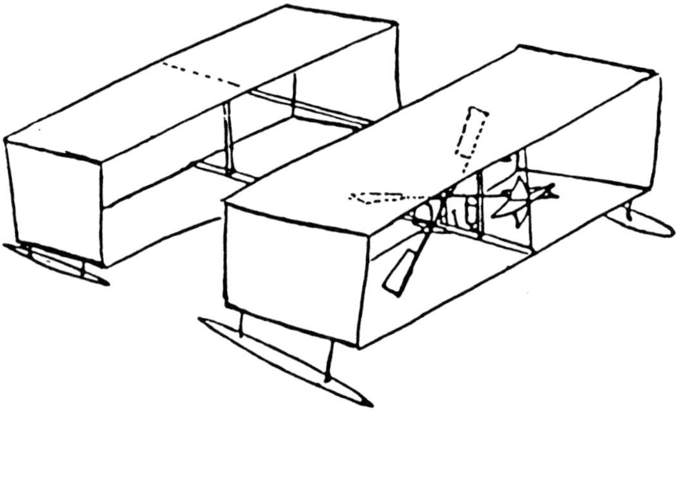

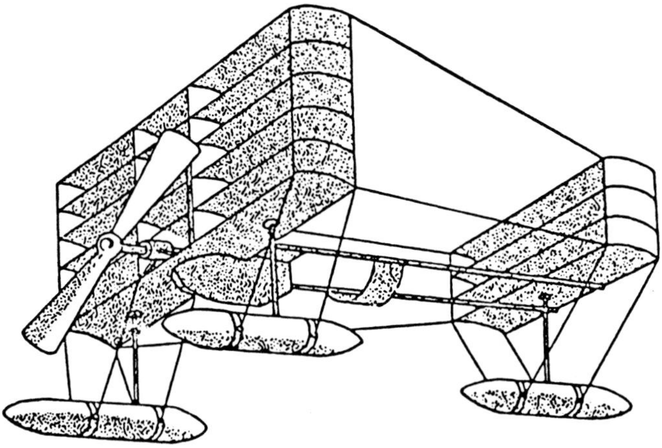

Figure 76. The steam-driven model floatplane made by Lawrence Hargrave in 1902. The wing plan used by Phillips is a feature of this machine.

application of the 'flying wing' concept (see figs. 77 and 78). The machine was demonstrated for the first time at Montesson on 3 March 1906 and it made four other flights during that year at that location and at Issy in the July, August and October. The best distance flown on these occasions was one of 79 ft after which the machine crashed.

The *Vuia No. 1* was not a large machine; it had a wing area of 215.3 sq. ft, and weighed 531 lb fully laden. It was fitted with the

Figure 77. The strange 'flying wing' aircraft built by Trajan Vuia in 1906. It was powered by the equally curious Serpollet carbonic acid gas motor.

Figure 78. Close-up view of Trajan Vuia's machine.

Serpollet 25 hp carbonic acid gas engine which drove a special fabric-covered propeller made by Victor Tatin. This strange engine could have worked in two ways. The simplest would have been to obtain small cylinders of carbon dioxide, apply a certain amount of heat to deliquify the gas and feed it to the ordinary four-cylinder engine by means of a regulating valve. The other method would have been to have a vessel with an upper and a lower chamber, with sulphuric acid in the higher area dripping onto calcium carbonate in the lower one. This would have produced the necessary carbon dioxide, which would then have been put under pressure to run the engine. This could have been done with a hand pump to start, with the engine driving an auxiliary pump to keep pressure up whilst in flight. From fig. 78 it appears that the former method could have been used.

After the crash-landing in 1906 the machine was rebuilt and renamed the *Vuia No. 1 bis*, and its control system was altered. Previously the wing control was operated by a variable incidence system but, in the 'bis' version, a triangular elevator was added to sustain better climbing ability. There was less camber and increased chord on the wing to increase its area by 32 sq. ft. Up to March 1907 eight attempts were made at Issy and at Bagatelle but the maximum flight distance recorded was a short hop of about 33 ft. The aircraft was again modified after these episodes and renamed the *Vuia No. 2*. This time it was fitted with an Antoinette internal combustion engine but the results with this were as dismal as with those using the carbonic acid gas motor.

George Davidson

The study of bird flight, as we have seen, has always been the mainstay of aviation pioneers and many of them drew the wrong conclusions from their observations; so it was with George Davidson. He interpreted the mechanics of the flight of birds in a similar way to Edward Frost, thinking that the flapping of wings provided lift rather than propulsion. From this erroneous premise he went on to design a flying machine which was a 'mechanical appliance which, by a rotary movement, would attain the same result as the reciprocal action of the birds'.

In 1896, Davidson promulgated proposals for his 'air-car', which was a high-wing monoplane with wings of a deep section within which were housed twenty-two fans placed in the horizontal plane to provide vertical lift along the whole span of both wings. These fans, or 'lifters', as Davidson called them, were driven off a pulley system which in turn was driven from a central engine room located in the fuselage. The upper and lower surfaces of the wings were to be covered with netting, over which was attached a series of non-return flaps made from a framework covered with silk or celluloid. The idea of this system was to allow the fans to draw in air from beneath the craft and to expel it through the top surface of the wings in order to provide lift; this enabled vertical flight to be achieved, and therefore when sufficient height had been attained, the fans were stopped and the flaps closed to ensure that a long glide could be made. From this method of propulsion the aeroplane flew along a 'saw-tooth' trajectory, with vertical lift off the airfield to the requisite height, then a long glide, another lift and glide and so on until the final glide allowed it to land! All of this was laid down in Davidson's specification of 6 June, 1896 (Brit. Pat. No. 12469), which was sealed on 5 June the following year.

Davidson always thought big and his plan called for an 'air-car' with a wingspan of 100 ft, an overall length of 45 ft and a double-deck fuselage 14 ft in height and 10 ft wide. This machine was to weigh 'upwards of 7½ tons' and, as well as the machinery and crew, some twenty passengers were to be accommodated. It was hoped that a useful lift of 10 tons could be generated with the system. A sectional front elevation and an overhead plan view are shown in fig. 79.

Davidson formed the Air-car Construction Syndicate Ltd with a declared capital of £20,000. On 1 November 1897 this syndicate made an agreement with its proprietor to purchase all patent rights and other interests demonstrated in the British patent. From this start a consulting engineer, W.L. Hamilton, was hired to design the airframe and later, in 1898, another expert, W.G. Walker, was approached to test the propellers. Walker examined twenty-eight of these fans of 2, 3 and 4 ft in diameter and tested them variously, at speeds between 500 and 2,800 rpm. From 3,000 results he concluded that 'lifters could be constructed capable of raising themselves, together with the weight of their driving machinery and appendages, up into the air'. A prospectus was issued in August 1898 which claimed: 'The successful machine should be completed in about nine months.' It also said that, after completion, when the first successful voyage had been made, 'the patents may be sold to a large company, resulting in an immediate return of at least £1,000 for each £10 invested in the present Syndicate'.

Unfortunately, the 'air-car' never materialized, and presumably, the Syndicate was wound up.

However, Davidson was not all hype, for in a lecture to the Aeronautical Society of Great Britain on 24 June 1898, he predicted air warfare, the siting of large airports near major cities and the ABC Airways Guide.

In 1906 Davidson returned to aviation with new proposals. His new project was for an intercontinental multi-passenger airliner driven by

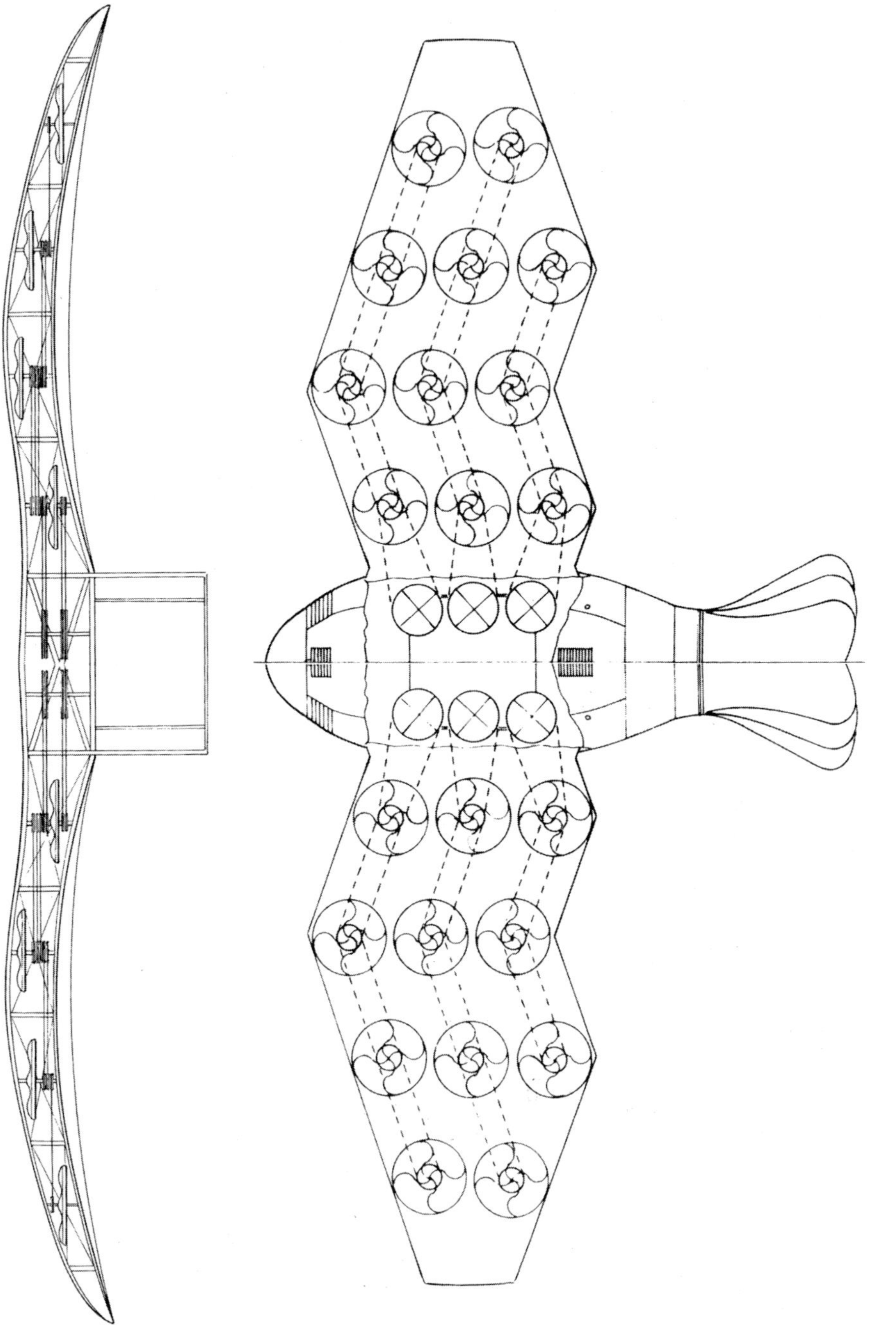

Figure 79. Front sectional elevation and overhead plan view of George Davidson's air-car of 1896–9.

the vertical lift method previously employed. A letter to *The Times* on 24 January 1906 from Alliot Verdun Roe spurred Davidson to contact him about the possibilities of powered heavier-than-air flight and he employed him to produce drawings for the new craft. Information about this aircraft was published in the *Automotor Journal* of 14 July 1906 and although the vertical 'lifters' were to be used, a different style of flight was proposed. The deep arched wings of the 'air-car' were apparent in the new design but instead of the multiplicity of 'lifters' within the wingspaces, each main spar had a vertical spindle at its tip, on which rotated a large, 120-vaned fan 30 ft in diameter and having a free space of 7 ft radius from its centre. The outer part of the 'lifter' protruded from beneath the wing and each fan was driven by its own steam engine located in the central engine room. Now the method of propulsion was by vertical lift at the outset and when the desired height was achieved the 'lifters' were tilted forwards or backwards a few degrees to maintain flight in either direction. Steering was by the variation of the relative speeds of each steam engine and by the use of a front-mounted rudder, or 'beak' as Davidson named it.

Just after Roe had commenced his drawings, Davidson managed to interest Lord Armstrong of Sir W.G. Armstrong-Whitworth & Co., the Newcastle shipbuilders, and he undertook to finance the work. Davidson decided to construct the machine in the USA and, together with Roe, he established a headquarters at Nichol's Castle, Montclair, near Denver. Soon after their arrival, Roe was despatched back to the UK to prepare more drawings for a new patent. On 25 January 1907 Brit. Pat. No. 1960 was applied for, and it was sealed on 23 January 1908.

Davidson's new syndicate was incorporated in America with a declared capital of $1 million in $1 shares and half of which was refunded to Lord Armstrong in respect of his advance. Another 100,000 shares were offered at 50¢ each as an incentive to raise an immediate $50,000. The prospectus published in the USA carried an impression of a huge 100 ton aircraft that would be able to carry 100 passengers from New York to Chicago in three hours at a cost of $10 each! By 22 October 1907 the machine was wheeled out in a partially constructed state (see fig. 80) and was seen to be somewhat smaller than the prospectus implied. Its 'lifters' had a diameter of 27 ft 8 in and comprised 110 vanes each. The distance between their vertical axes was 40 ft and the overall span was 67 ft. The body was designed to be 13 ft high and 8 ft wide with an overall length of 60 ft. The power plant was to consist of two 50 hp Stanley steam engines.

Catastrophe struck during a test at Denver on the 8 May 1908, when the boiler was forced so much after lift-off that it exploded and

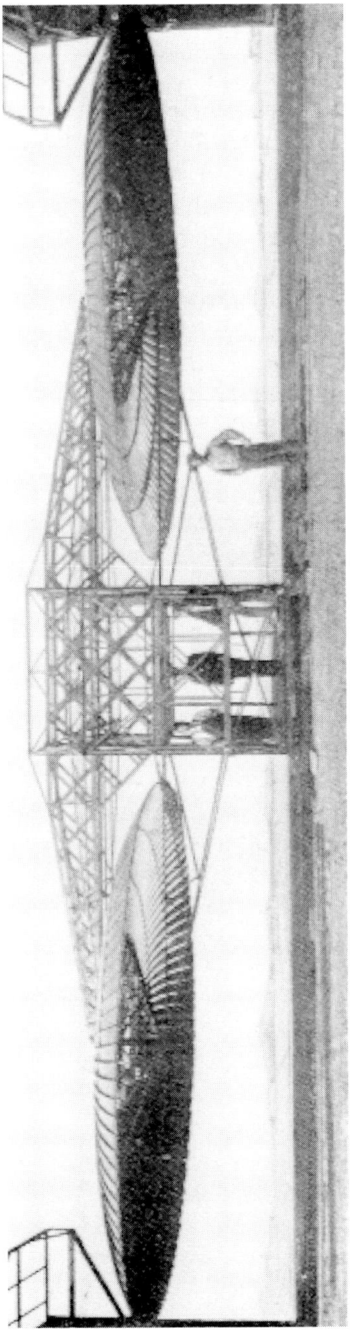

Figure 80. George Davidson's second attempt at making a flying machine. Photographed during construction at Montclair, Colorado, USA on 22 October 1907.

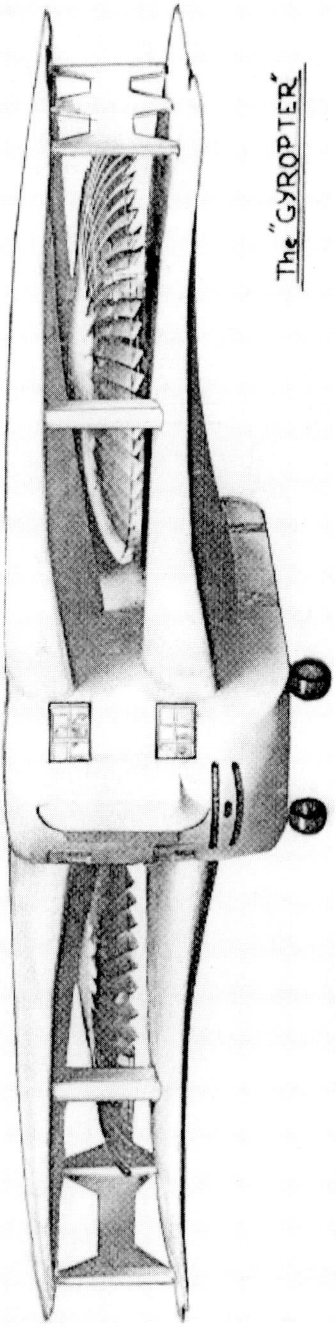

Figure 81. A drawing of the gyropter model that was exhibited at the model aircraft exhibition at Olympia in 1911 by George Davidson.

wrecked the whole machine. It seems that Davidson had claimed that a lift of 3 tons had been achieved with engines of 80 to 100 hp, but another report stated that a lift of only 1 ton had been accomplished using an old 10 hp Stanley engine. The accident spelled the end of the experiments in Colorado and Davidson returned home.

This was not the end of the Davidson saga however, for later in 1908 he set about building a new machine which he named the 'gyropter', a word which later came into the English language. He entered this machine for the prize of £10,000 offered by the *Daily Mail* for a flight from London to Manchester. He announced that his craft would weigh 4 tons, have engines of over 100 hp, carry twelve passengers and do the trip in three hours. Drawings of the gyropter revealed that its method of working was substantially similar to the American project: it had the double-deck fuselage, a port and starboard rotary 'lifter', the front 'beak' rudder and three biplane wings mounted one behind the other.

Davidson established new premises at Taplow in Buckinghamshire and with a team of workers, he commenced construction. In June 1910 a new company was promoted as Davidson's Gyropter Flying Machine Ltd, registered to acquire 'certain patents and rights relating to flying machines'. Its declared capital was a mere £250 in 1d shares. A prospectus was issued calling for 'considerable funds' and stating that the fuselage framework and main spars had been completed; Davidson also claimed that he had already spent £12,500 in twenty-seven years of study and experiment and that basic experimentation had been successful. He invited prospective investors to view the machine by appointment and he predicted that with a weight of upwards of 6 tons, and a lifting power of 4 tons, the gyropter would travel at a speed far in excess of any aeroplane. In November a report from the journal *Flight*

Figure 82. Section through the fuselage of the 'Gyropter'.

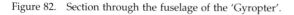

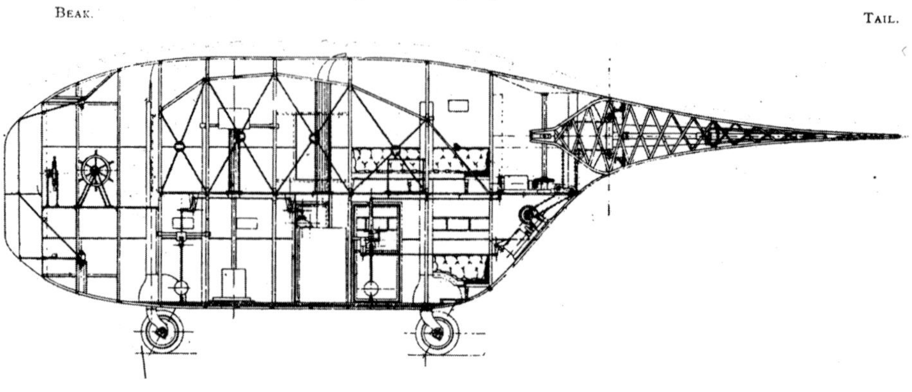

visited the Taplow site, only to say of the machine: 'It is unfinished and is likely to remain unfinished unless others who are as interested in this particular problem as Mr Davidson himself come forward to his financial assistance'.

The Taplow 'gyropter' had smaller 'lifters' of 26 ft 10 in diameter driven through bevel gearing and shafting by two 'special' Stanley steam engines; the flight method was to be the same as in the Colorado machine. *Flight* again reported on progress in their issue of 25 February 1911, describing the scene in the workshop as 'a veritable forest of timber' and that one of the 60 hp Stanley engines was in place with its transmission linked to a 'lifter'. At about this time Davidson showed a model at a Model Aircraft Exhibition at Olympia (see fig. 81), and this apparently survives, having been lent to the Science Museum by the Royal Aeronautical Society in 1928.

Figure 83. Plan view of Davidson's 'Gyropter' showing the three pairs of biplane wings and the rotary 'lifters'.

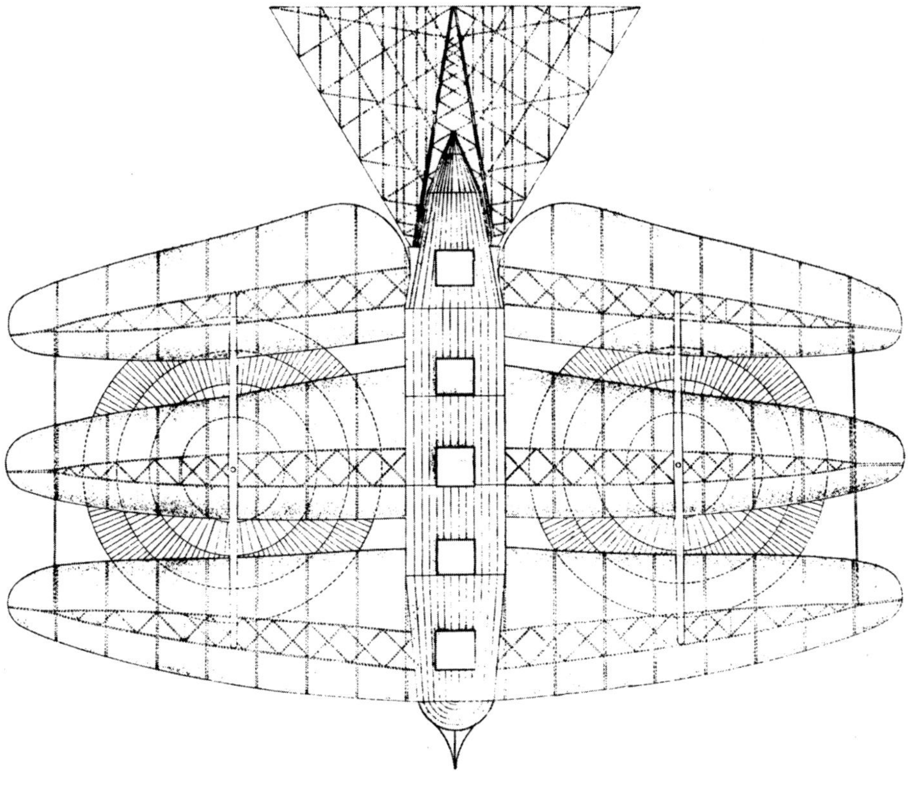

More prospectuses were issued in March 1911 telling investors that the weight of the machine was 'upwards of 7 tons' and that it would carry twenty passengers at a 'speed far in excess of 100 mph'. It seems, however, that financial desperation had set in, for the last mention of the 'gyropter' came in the December 1911 issue of *The Aero*, when a reader said that he had seen it 'in an advanced stage towards completion' and that it would have a wingspan of 76 ft and be 66 ft in length. It was never completed, however, like all of Davidson's efforts. However, it is fair to say that the vast task that he attempted has even today not come to fruition, for a vertical take-off intercontinental airliner is still only speculation.

Davidson was rewarded in some way for his efforts for he was admitted as a member of the Aeronautical Society of Great Britain on 6 April 1909.

H.H. Groves

Groves was an exponent of the monotube or 'flash' steam system and he applied his ideas to model aircraft with a great degree of success. He commenced his work just before the outbreak of the First World War. He is known to have made and flown two steam-powered aeroplanes, a monoplane and a biplane, both of the 'canard' or tail-first configuration and both described in a 1913 issue of the *Model Engineer*. Groves continued his experiments and his work right up to the 1930s, and another account of steam aircraft power plants was published in the same journal in 1936.

The first Groves aeroplane was the monoplane shown in fig. 86. This had the monotube steam generator and its allied burner housed in the perforated tube located between the two planes. A combined fuel and water tank was slung beneath the boiler and this was pressurized using a bicycle pump. The boiler worked on the once-through parameter with the water being 'flashed' into steam on its journey through the labyrinth and being exhausted to atmosphere from the engine. The engine itself was a single-acting horizontally opposed unit (see figs 84 and 85); it was all very simple, but also very light in weight. A person named F.W. Westmoreland witnessed a flight of this monoplane on Sunday, 26 September 1916 and confirmed that it performed superbly, but that unfortunately during the execution of some aerobatic manoeuvres it hit a bank and the airframe was badly damaged.

Groves also made the biplane shown in fig. 87 which was fitted with an identical power unit. Another steam aircraft plant was described in 1936, a double-acting geared engine being fed from a similar generator to that used in the earlier versions.

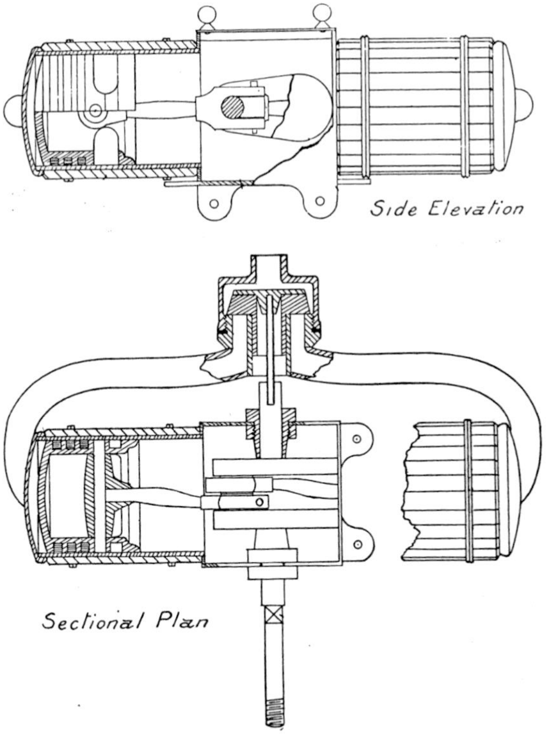

Figure 84. Line drawing of the horizontally opposed power unit used by H.H. Groves in the 1913 models.

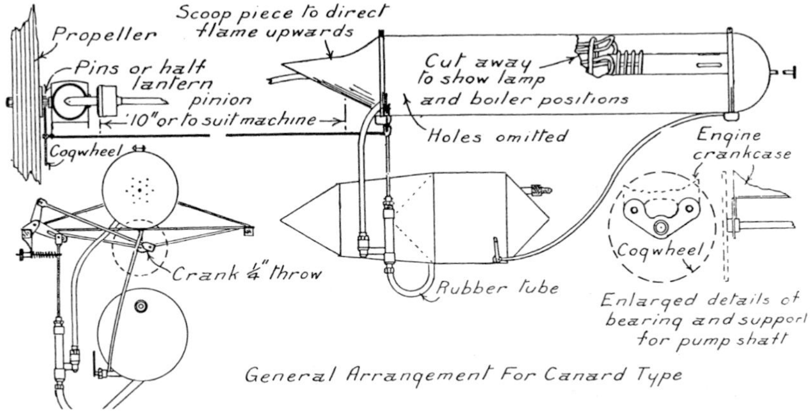

Figure 85. Diagram of the installation of Groves's steam power unit in a pusher aeroplane.

Figure 86. The Groves steam monoplane of 1913.

Figure 87. The biplane version of the Groves machine.

The specifications of these diminutive steam engines give some idea of how small working engines may be made. The horizontally opposed unit which was first seen in 1913 had a bore of 0.625 in and a stroke of 1 in, and it weighed 3½ oz. The whole plant was the result of two years of experiment which was not without its hazards. The initial plan was to generate steam in a water tube boiler and to plot thrust and other

Figure 88. Powerplant of the biplane model made by H.H. Groves

performance. When the experimental plant was operated the initial thrust at the propeller was 4 oz, which rose to 9 oz, at which point the fuel reservoir exploded and terminated the test. The 9 oz thrust was insufficient for the purpose of flight as the whole of the steam plant weighed 24 oz. Further experiments were made using the monotube system of steam generation together with a feed pump driven off the engine, but these were inconclusive because the delivery of the feed water was intermittent. Even so, the engine performance was much enhanced. After many changes of material, from copper to steel etc., suitable metals were found and the unit then managed to produce a thrust of 12 oz, which was judged to be just sufficient to make a trial flight possible. When everything was finalized the engine/boiler unit weighed 2 lb and the total weight of engine and airframe was 3 lb 13 oz, with average thrust available of 20 oz. Four flights were made and three were successful; a height of 100 ft was achieved on the final flight. The aeroplane used was the monoplane shown in fig. 86.

The later, double-acting geared engine made by Groves was even smaller than the 1913 unit for it had a bore and stroke of 0.250 in by

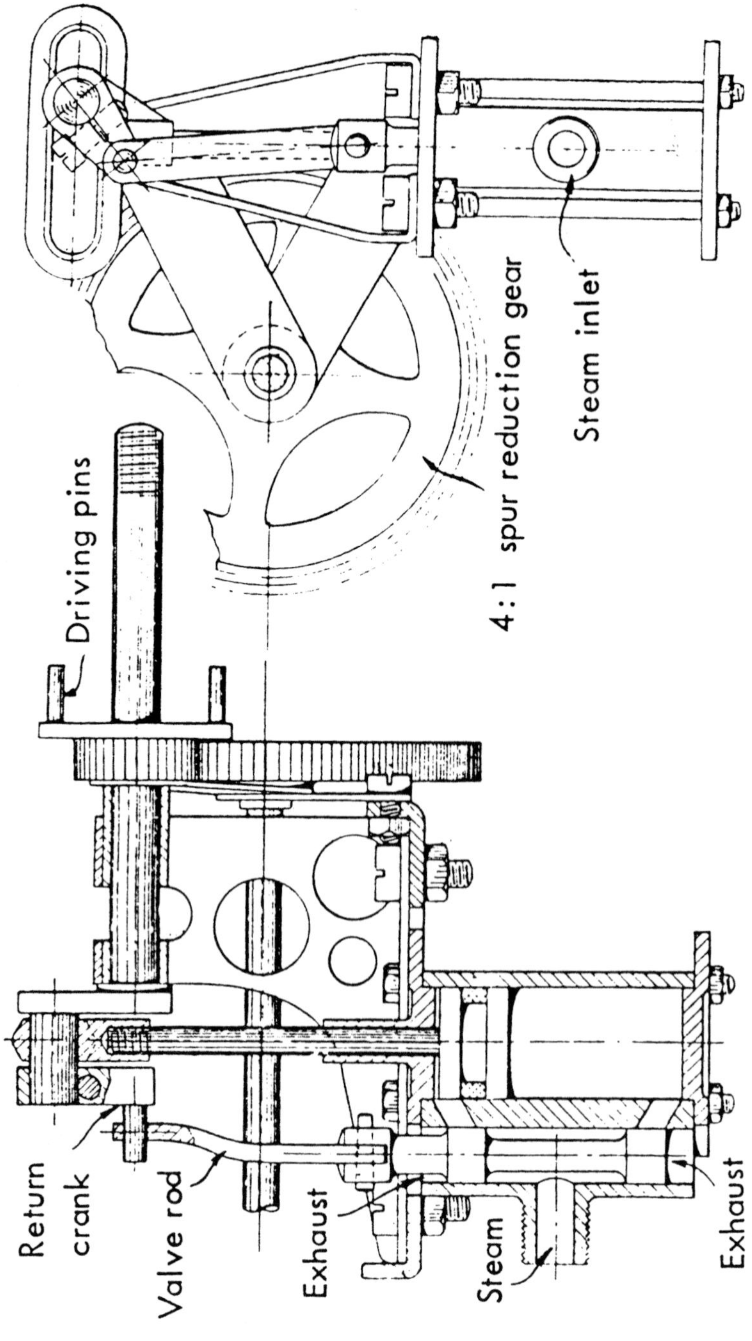

Figure 89. The later double-acting aeronautical steam engine designed by H.H. Groves in 1936.

0.4375 in; it was fitted with a piston valve of 0.125 in bore by 0.125 in stroke. With its boiler and ancillaries (see fig. 89), the plant weighed 5 oz, making it probably the smallest steam aero-engine ever built. After Groves few enthusiasts concentrated on producing steam engines for model aircraft and tended to concentrate on hydroplanes. The idea of steam-driven model aeroplanes became dormant.

William J. and George Besler

In the full-sized area the heavier-than-air machine was soon to become a reality. The original work of the Doble brothers, Abner and Warren, in California had produced some very lightweight engines which had good power outputs. These engines were fitted to a number of passenger cars and, in the mid-1930s to steam wagons and railcars. Unfortunately all their work was really of an on-going experimental nature and the results were of more scientific than commercial value.

In the 1930s two other brothers came upon the scene in America, who were instrumental in achieving the first sustained, controlled and manned heavier-than-air steam powered flight. The Besler brothers were the sons of the Chairman of the Central Railroad of New Jersey

Figure 90. The Travelair biplane converted to steam power by the Besler brothers in 1933. This aircraft made the first manned, controlled and sustained flight on 20 April of that year.

and they were to become important figures in the field of steam engineering using monotube boilers and lightweight engines for many applications: specialized stationary plant, one or two automotive installations and small-boat power. There was also a futuristic 1,000 hp steam railcar which was supplied to the New York, Newhaven & Hartford Railroad in 1937.

However, it is for the application of a small vee-twin steam plant to a Travelair biplane in 1933 that they became famous in aviation circles. They knew the Doble brothers and it is thought that they worked together. When the Dobles relinquished their purpose-built facility in Emeryville, California, the Beslers took it over as it was eminently suitable for their use because they were building the same type of product.

On 20 April 1933 William J. Besler demonstrated his steam-driven aircraft to members of the US National Aeronautic Association at the San Francisco Bay Airdrome. The aeroplane performed excellently, for it was entirely noiseless in operation with only the whirring of the tips of the airscrew being heard, whilst it was capable of maintaining a

Figure 91. The boiler and control unit on the Besler steam aircraft.

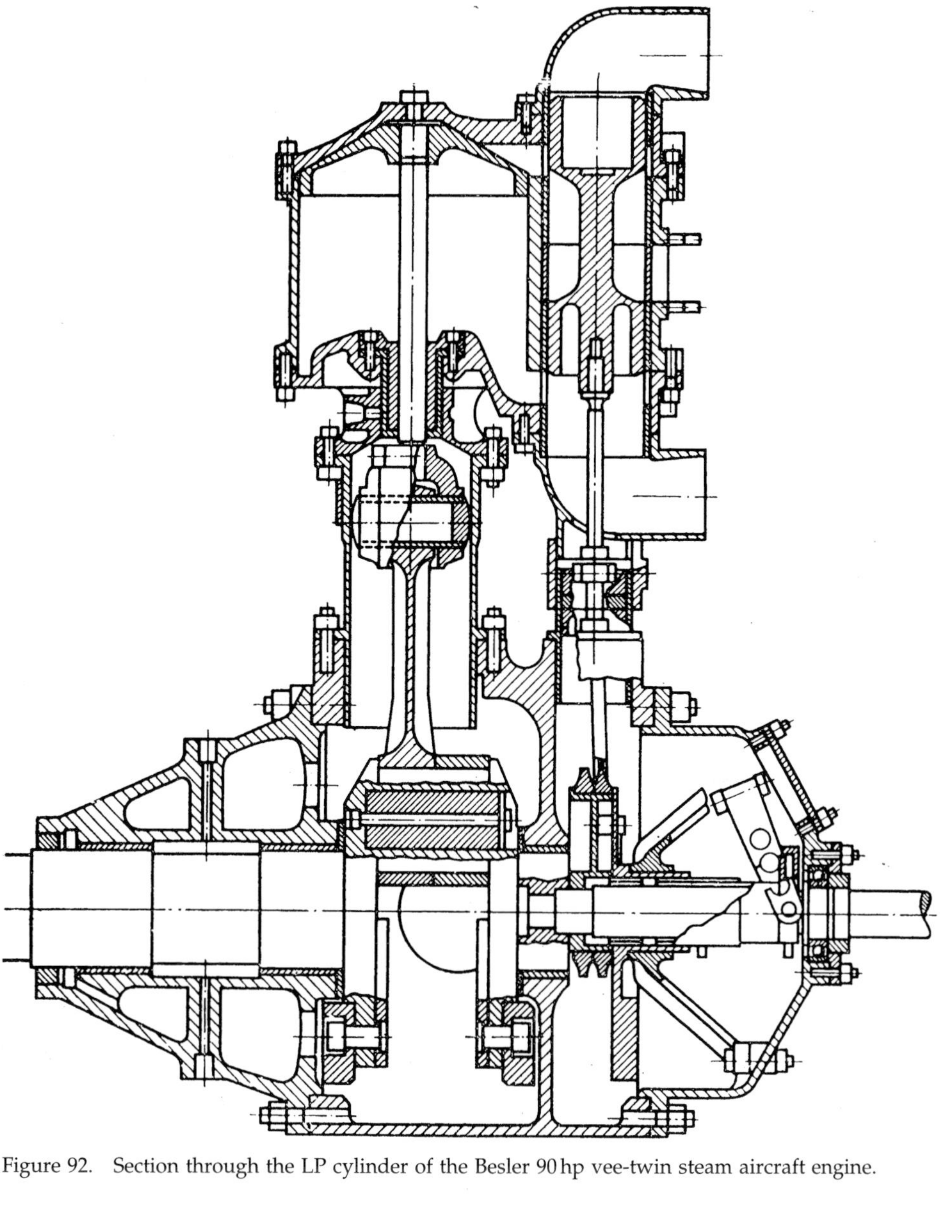

Figure 92. Section through the LP cylinder of the Besler 90 hp vee-twin steam aircraft engine.

speed of 100 mph in flight. William Besler took off, made a short flight of several minutes and landed safely, making this the first proper flight with a steam-powered machine other than an airship; eighty-one years after the flight of Henri Giffard.

Soon after the flight, the steam equipment was removed and it was all taken to the Emeryville factory for storage to reappear in the guise of a marine installation in a US Navy personnel picquet boat in October 1958 where it was used until September 1959 for tests by the US Navy Engineering Experimental Station at Annapolis in Maryland.

The power unit (see figs. 91 and 92) consisted of the vee-twin engine, a compound unit with its cylinders set at 90 degrees; it had bores of 3 in hp and 5½ in lp with a common stroke of 4 in. In the aircraft it produced 90 shp but this was up-rated to 115 shp when installed in the boat. A monotube boiler supplied steam at a pressure of 650 psi with a superheat temperature of 399° C and the whole outfit had condensing gear; a pressurized burner system ignited by means of a spark plug and using ordinary fuel oil enabled steam to be raised within about one minute. This Besler steam generation unit was similar to others made in several sizes, with some of the larger ones weighing some 3,600 lb. The weight of the engine was 273 lb, whilst the steam generation system weighed 789 lb – a total of under ½ ton when installed in the boat. It is believed that the boiler unit was lighter when used in the aeroplane and that only a small amount of fuel was carried, hence the shortness of the flight.

This flight is noteworthy because it showed that the steam aeroplane was a viable proposition, and also that in light aircraft there was no need for variable-pitch airscrews, owing to the engine cut-off and the fact that the steam engine was easily reversible.

Once the Besler brothers had made this inaugural flight, one would have thought that they would capitalize on their achievement but, there was no further activity by the Emeryville firm; the Besler Corporation concentrated its efforts on manufacturing compact monotube steam plants for commercial purposes.

Other Activity in Steam Aviation in the Middle of the Twentieth Century

The fact that the Besler brothers were successful with steam-powered flight seemed to act as an incentive for others to become interested in the challenge.

In the mid-1930s the Great Lakes Aircraft Corporation of America entered into an agreement with the General Electric Company to research the possibility of manufacturing a large steam turbine installation for flying boats. The result of this association was the design of the propeller-driven machine shown (see fig 93). A steam power unit of 2,300 hp was mooted using a LaMont steam generator which was of the water-tube type. This boiler was a very efficient producer of steam and it featured an air pre-heater, a blower which was driven by an electric motor to induce primary combustion air, a nest of alloy steel tubing arranged in the form of a cylinder for water and steam flow, and a superheater. This steam generator could be started at the touch of a button in the cockpit when the fuel was pressurized and the blower started with ignition effected by a spark plug. In service the boiler could evaporate 9.5 tons per hour at a pressure of 1,029 psi and a superheat value of 540° C. The steam generator was mounted within the fuselage just behind the flight deck with its exhaust pipe protruding just in front of the wing mounting struts. The line drawing shows the method of operation with the blower forward of the boiler shell and the fuel and water ancillary modules just aft; steam piping and condensate return is routed via the support struts.

Figure 93. The Great Lakes Air Corporation steam plant with wing-mounted turbine and condenser.

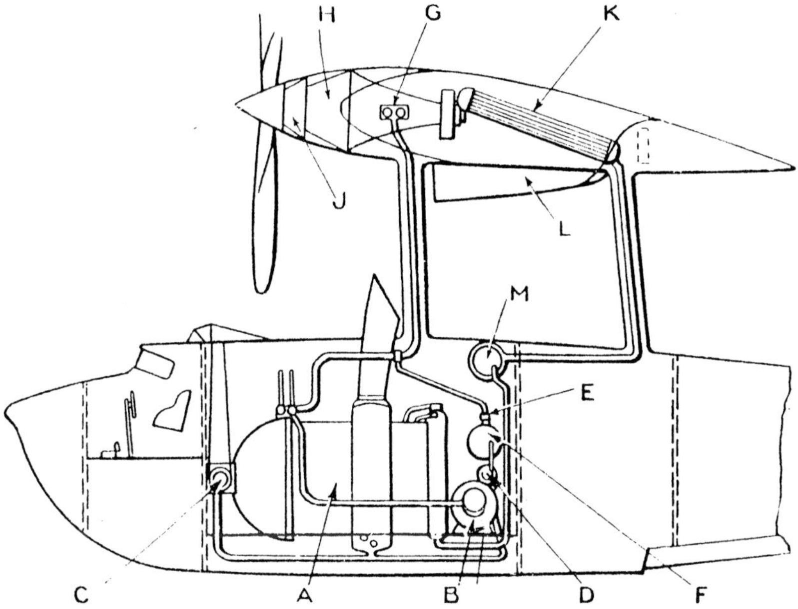

A. Steam generator.
B. Fuel supply unit.
C. Blower.
D. Feed water.
E. Ejector.
F. Steam line condensate collector.
G. Valve.
H. Turbine.
J. Reduction gear.
K. Condenser.
L. Air scoop.
M. Condensate collector.

The General Electric Co. of Schenectady, NY, were well versed in turbine technology, having been in the marine business for many years before this foray into aeronautics. Their turbines were mainly of the impulse variety and from the shape of the casing shown in the drawing, it would appear that this installation was similar in style to the GEC main impulse marine type.

The ceiling height for operation of this power plant was calculated at about 5,000 ft and its efficiency was claimed to be 23 per cent, with a fuel consumption of 9½ oz per hp. The writer has no doubt that the engine installation was actually built, but whether or not it was ever put into a flying boat, let alone flown, is a different matter.

Another interesting development which occurred in 1938 was the unitary steam turbine assembly designed by Aero Turbines Ltd of London (see fig. 94). This machine was a complete and integrated steam power plant which contained all the elements necessary for a compact installation, say in the fuselage of an aeroplane. It consisted of a steam generator that rotated, a turbine with rotor and stator, a combustion chamber and a condenser. The diagram, shown in section, demonstrates the method of working, with the boiler and the turbine rotating in opposite directions; the machine is started using an electric motor which pumps fuel and water into the unit and ignites the fuel/air mixture with a sparking plug – the starting revolutions continue until sufficient steam has been raised to enable the turbine to take over. Although steam to about 25 psi could be raised within sixty-five seconds this initial rotation was of very short duration; moreover, this turbine was not fussy about fuel and distillates would have been very suitable. It probably could have operated on marine diesel fuel. The original test unit was of 30 hp and a weight-to-power figure was given of 2 lb per hp to make an all-up weight of just 60 lb. Other sizes were offered and a unit of 2,000 hp working at 2,205 psi could achieve a turbine speed of 10,000 rpm with the boiler rotating in the opposite direction at 5,000 rpm – this type weighed about 4,000 lb, which was quite heavy for an aero-engine. Although it was conceived for a multitude of different services and uses, the makers did suggest its use in aviation; but it is not thought, however, that one was ever fitted to an aircraft.

Another application for steam turbines in aviation was as an adjunct to use waste heat in aircraft power plants, to operate as a blower system in early jets and to enhance aerodynamic characteristics in wing sections. Two such systems have been described in the technical press of the 1930s and 1940s but neither seems to have been adopted successfully.

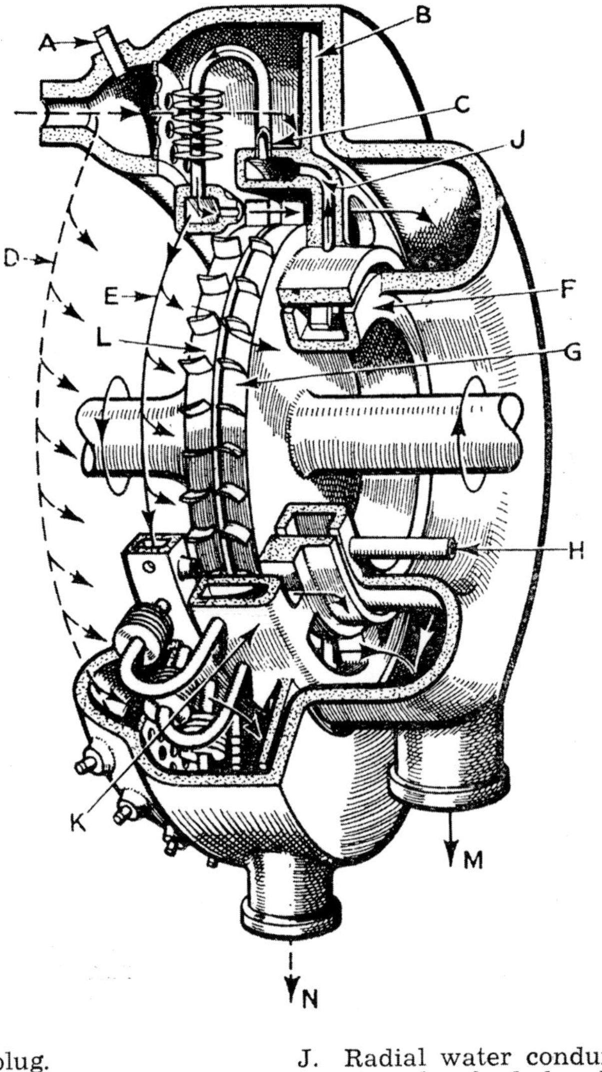

A. Ignition plug.
B. Insulating wall.
C. Atomiser.
D. Path of flame.
E. Path of steam.
F. Centrifugal Pump.
G. Reaction disc.
H. Water inlet.
J. Radial water conduits.
K. Annular feed chamber, U-tubes and nozzle ring integral with reaction disc.
L. Turbine rotor.
M. Exhaust steam to condenser.
N. Combustion effluent.

Figure 94. Steam turbine assembly designed by Aero Turbines.

The first steam turbine auxiliary arrangement was outlined in a patent filed on 16 July 1938 by the well-known inventor, Igor Sikorsky and two colleagues, M.E. Gulharev and R.W. Griswold (US Pat. No. 2252528 of 1938, sealed in 1941). This patent was assigned to the United Aircraft Corporation and its specification featured a normal radial aero-engine which was enclosed within a cowling to drive the plane's airscrew. However, its cooling air was drawn in by the suction of a blower driven by an exhaust-gas turbine using the spent gases from the main power unit; the air thus sucked in was routed to a chamber in the wing section where it was used for de-icing. On the same shaft as the gas turbine there was a steam turbine driven off steam generated in an exhaust gas boiler; this steam was condensed for re-use whilst the blower took air from the leading-edge chamber to a duct which distributed it along the trailing edge of the wing. In this way all the waste heat generated from the radial engine's exhaust was gainfully used. It is worth noting that the exhaust from the radial engine drove turbines in two different ways: as a form of turbo-charger, and by using waste heat from the products of combustion to provide steam. Two important questions about this system – 'How much did it weigh?' and, 'Did its complexity outweigh its usefulness?' – were not answered at the time and, therefore, the system does not appear to have been used commercially.

The other steam turbine system was actually applied to an aircraft that was made during the Second World War in France. In April 1942 a report was made concerning an experimental jet-propelled aeroplane which was being constructed at the Bréguet Aircraft Works in Toulouse. This machine was similar in style to the well-known Caproni-Campini which used a normal aircraft engine to force ducted air through a jet orifice in the tail. However, the Bréguet plane, which was designed by R. Ledue, used a steam turbine power unit to do the same thing. No details seem to be available about the boiler and the condensing system but the turbine itself was said to be of the Vuia type (possibly designed by Trajan Vuia for he was very much alive at the time), which ran at 3,000 rpm with a steam pressure of 1,910 psi to give an estimated output of 1,200 hp. Perhaps the condensing unit was placed in the ducted air-stream to provide extra heat for propulsion, and, perhaps boilers of the monotube variety were situated in the wings; it was an interesting project but the writer has been unable to discover more about it. The estimated speed of this aircraft was 310 mph but it has not been established whether or not it actually flew.

After the Second World War there is little of any real developments in steam aviation, although at one stage in the late 1950s, the Goodyear

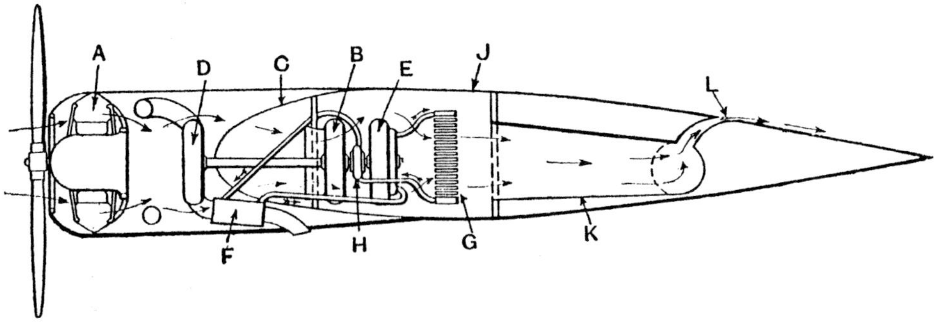

A. Radial engine.
B. Centrifugal blower.
C. Wing leading-edge air chamber.
D. Exhaust gas turbine.
E. Steam turbine.
F. Exhaust heated boiler.
G. Condenser.
H. Water pump.
J. Mid-wing air chamber
K. Air duct.
L. Spanwise slot.

Figure 95. Steam turbine auxiliary system devised by Igor Sikorsky for the United Aircraft Corporation just before the Second World War.

Aircraft Corporation made a statement concerning a huge airship, to be driven by nuclear power, which would be capable of speeds up to 900 mph, and would cruise at an altitude of 10,000 ft! This vessel was supposed to be used for anti-submarine patrols and it was to be fitted with a large double-decker, control gondola that was 86 ft in length. A crew of twenty-four men would be required to fly it, and of course, it would have to be propelled by steam as this is the only means of harnessing atomic power!

At more or less the same times as the Goodyear airship was mooted another firm in the USA was developing steam power for use in space. A company named Vickers, operating in Torrance, near Los Angeles, were advertising that they had invented a 'hydrogen engine' for use as an auxiliary power source for lighting, heating etc. in manned satellites. The engine that was developed (see fig. 96) was a three-cylinder radial unit that worked on steam generated by the controlled combustion of hydrogen and oxygen in a vessel known as a 'combustor' using spark ignition. This engine only weighed 15 lb and it produced 40 hp at 8,000 rpm. An experimental programme was undertaken in 1960 and, apparently, encouraging results were obtained. A variable cut-off system was employed which varied from 4 to 30 per cent of the stroke and the gas or steam which was supplied to the intake had controlled variations in the proportions of hydrogen and oxygen. The variations in cut-off were controlled by means of a graduated opening of poppet valves actuated by one cam on the crankshaft and another driven by a governer; the poppet valves were driven by push-rods. A working

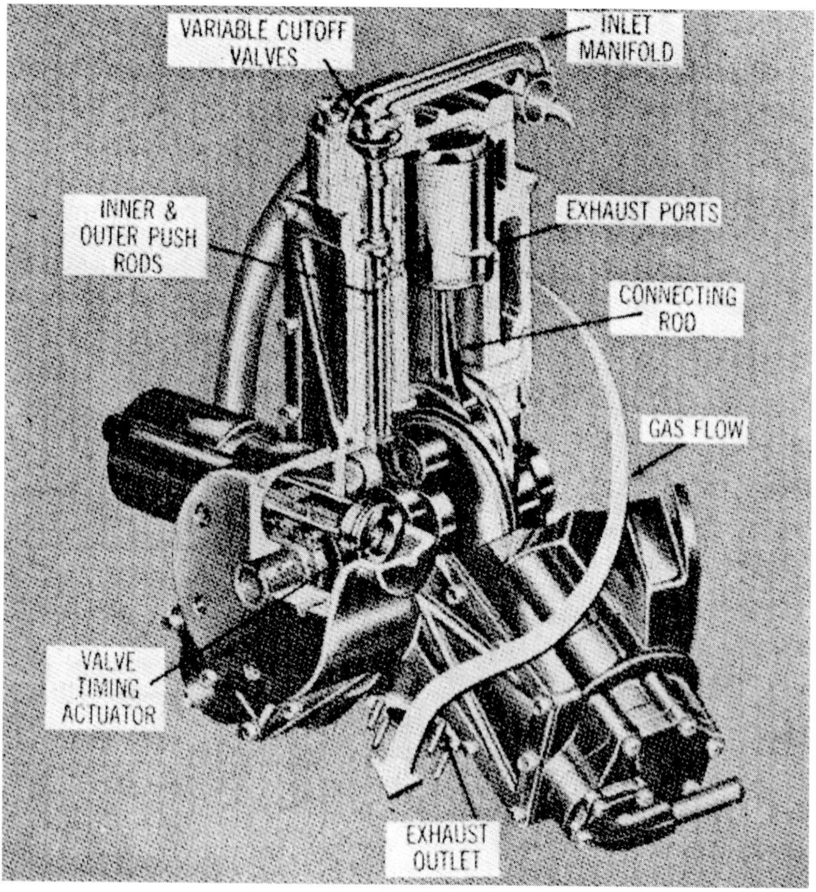

Figure 96. The three-cylinder radial engine designed for use in space by Vickers of Torrance, California, USA.

pressure of 765 psi was given with gas inlet temperatures from 21 to 454° C. Using a single-cylinder test rig a fuel consumption of 1.6 lb per hp/hr was achieved. What happened to the commercial application of this engine has not been revealed.

The Nuclear Steam Airship

Professor Francis Morse of Boston University, USA, who headed the Morse Committee which investigated the hydrocarbon emissions problems in road vehicles in the late 1960s, made a novel suggestion regarding long-distance passenger and cargo air travel in 1966. He formed a team of scientists to investigate the possibilities of his proposal and

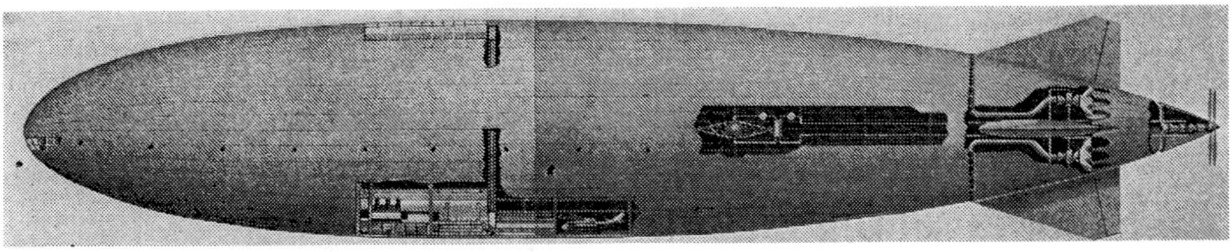

Figure 97. Nuclear airship proposed by Professor Francis Morse.

came up with the idea of a large airship that would be propelled by steam using nuclear fuel.

The purpose of this design was to conserve fossil fuels with a view to reducing the emission of carbon dioxide and to provide cheap and efficient air transport which could compete with water-borne transport on a 'cost per ton-mile' basis. Realizing that all conventional aircraft require a large store of fuel on board, which consumes energy as well as reducing the payload, they investigated the use of nuclear power. Despite the fact that some extra weight would have to be carried in the form of radiation shielding, it was felt at the time that this would not add as much weight as petroleum fuel.

Figure 97 shows a layout of the proposed airship. The passenger accommodation is on the left, together with a special hangar to house a sixteen-seater aircraft alongside it. The nuclear reactor was to have been encased within a 12 ft diameter sphere and steam from the associated boiler was fed to the turbine room aft, where the turbines would drive contra-rotating airscrews 60 ft in diameter. The proposed power output of this nuclear plant was to be in the region of 6,000 shp and its estimated weight 120,000 lb or 53½ tons! The envelop was to contain 14 million cu. ft of helium gas or twice the volume of that of the LZ-129 *Hindenburg*. Advances made since 1966 in nuclear technology may result in a lesser power plant weight, but the disposable payload weight might have inhibited unit costs per pound of cargo or per passenger when compared to, say, a Boeing 747. Moreover, even with modern, enhanced, navigational equipment this monster would have been very difficult to control, particularly in adverse weather conditions.

Ronald Whitehouse

After a period of stagnation in aerial steam navigation a startling story appeared in the London *Evening Standard* on 11 January 1990, which said: 'Inventor Ronnie Whitehouse is bidding to become a high-flying record breaker'. The article, which illustrated a Rutan aeroplane and the inventor displaying a small power unit, went on to state that Mr Whitehouse was attempting to break the world steam-powered speed record. The writer was then able to discover the background to this revelation.

In the early 1970s Whitehouse sought to improve the environment and minimise pollution by inventing a lightweight prime mover operated by steam, which would be able to use a wide range of fuels, some of which would be practically free from harmful emissions. He also envisaged that his engine could be suitable for aeronautical as well as land applications.

This new prime mover was given the name OPUS, an acronym which stood for 'orbital power systems', a name which reflects its mode of operation, for it is a rotary piston engine of very simple construction, having about fifteen components altogether; with the use of carbon fibre and other modern plastics it was also oil free. A prototype was made, which can be seen on colour section page 8. Whitehouse is shown demonstrating its size whilst sitting in the cockpit of a Rutan aeroplane. It is able to fit into a box not much larger than an attaché case and weighs about 22 lb. Soon after he unveiled this prototype it was entered as an exhibit at Eureka – Salon Mondial des Inventions in December 1974, where it was awarded both the Medaille de Vermeil and the Medaille d'or de Bruxelles for its novelty and presentation.

The method of working is interesting; from the schematic diagram shown in fig. 98 it will be seen that the power source may be divided into three sections: the steam-raising element, the electrics and control system and the power unit itself. It operates in a closed-circuit module which is controlled electronically. When the operator (or pilot) switches on the controls, the fuel and feed-water systems are actuated and the fuel is ignited in the combustion chamber to produce steam in a short space of time at a high degree of superheat. After steam has been raised to a significant pressure the closed-circuit system operates automatically and control is really effected by throttle opening alone. The steam generator is of the water-tube pattern, using thin-walled, small-bore tubing to ensure quick transfer of heat. This boiler element is encased in a stainless steel cylinder. An electrical generator, driven directly by the engine, provides power for the auxiliaries as well as the control electronics, which monitor such items as fuel flow to match steam mass and usage at any given time to ensure that the unit is not starved of steam input at any throttle opening. The novelty of this invention lies in the design of the rotary engine and the diversity of fuels that can be used, including kerosene (paraffin), methane, LPG, hydrogen, petrol, and 'eco-fuel', a low-cost gaseous fuel with a greater calorific value than ordinary petrol; this fuel is also part of the inventor's specification.

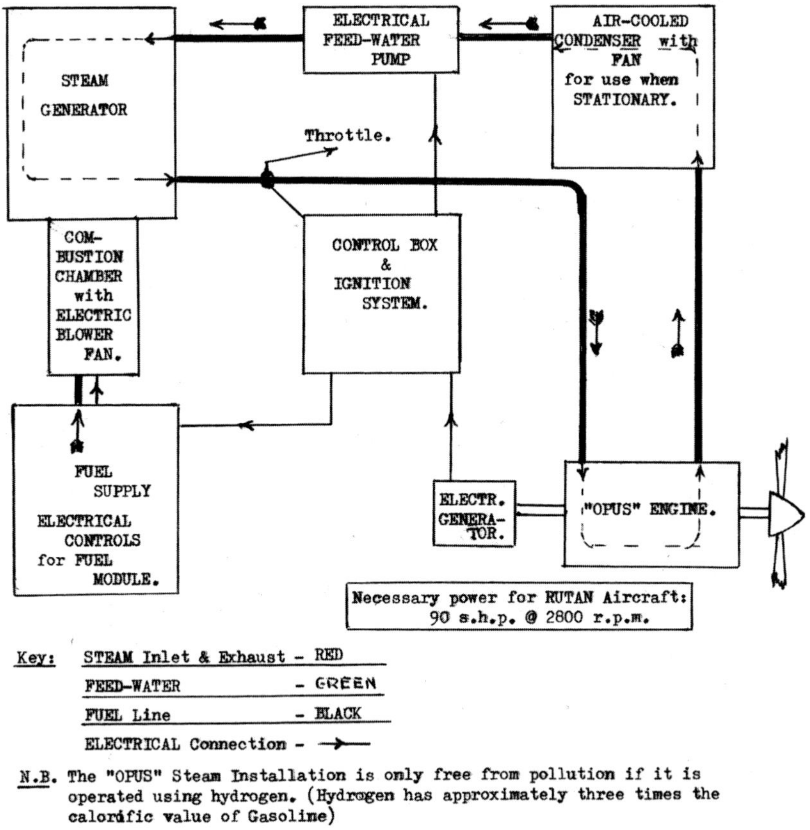

Figure 98. Diagrammatic layout of the OPUS steam power system in the Rutan aeroplane.

The lure of the world speed record for steam power attracted Whitehouse to consider installing the OPUS plant in an aeroplane and he formulated 'a world speed record attempt for silent, pollution-free flight with the revolutionary Rutan aircraft and the rotary "OPUS" engine'. However, invitations to sponsor this attempt as well as backing for the power system itself have not met with complete success, for although British Steel (now Corus) did donate special material to build the power plant, and Camden Enterprise expressed interest, the realization of capital has been an uphill struggle.

Nevertheless, the design is likely to be put into effect, for in America the Rutan Aircraft Factory Inc. of Mohave, California, make an aircraft kit which is eminently suitable for the purpose of OPUS installation.

The founders of the company, Burt and Richard Rutan, have built up a reputation for the design and sale of specialized kits, made from carbon-fibre and other 'space-age' materials, to build a radical 'canard' type of light aircraft; enthusiasts can assemble the kit to their own tastes and then install any power plant to suit their needs. The way the OPUS system fits into the Rutan fuselage is shown in fig. 99.

One of the notable feats using Rutan aeroplanes was the successful circumnavigation of the globe by Burt Rutan and Chuck Yeager in the Rutan Voyager in 1986. An article in *Air International* stated: 'Burt Rutan has designed a remarkable series of record-breaking aircraft of the last twenty years. Rutan's use of composite construction coupled with innovative use of canard low-drag air configurations has coupled long range with high speed to an unprecedented degree for such a small aircraft!' Everything is therefore in place for a record run; but sponsorship is the only component that is lacking. Since the early 1990s Whitehouse has tried to attract backers but has met with apathy.

Apart from the Rutan light aeroplane, an OPUS airship has been mooted, with an illustration of the craft (see fig. 100), and a description of its applications being included in the publicity material. The text

Figure 99. Schematic diagram of the OPUS aircraft installation.

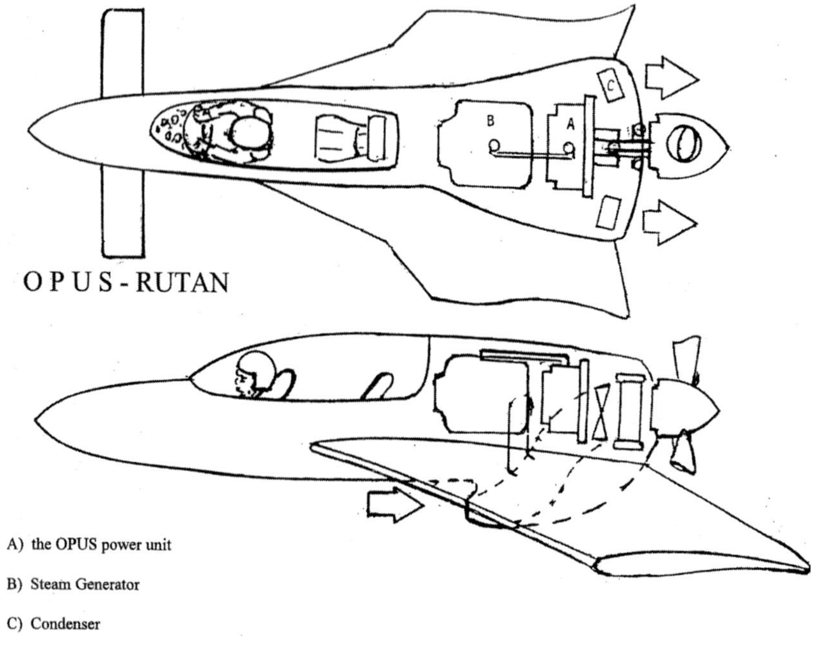

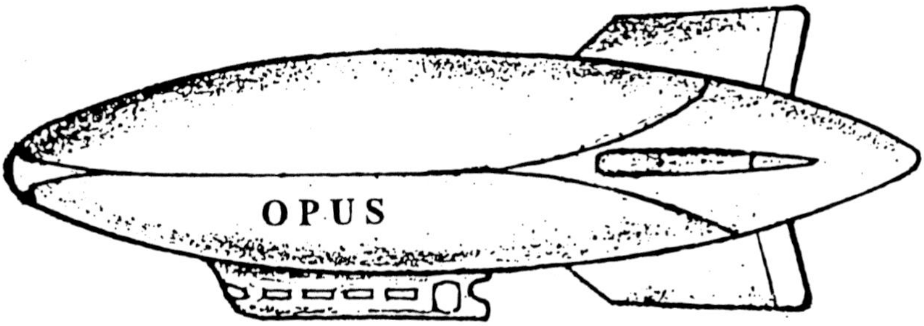

Figure 100. The OPUS airship proposed by R. Whitehouse.

stated that the OPUS engine with its high torque at low speeds, together with its high power-to-weight ratio, was ideally suited to the airship usage. It could hold the airship in a 'hove-to' position into the wind or be able to accelerate to full power for 'dash-speeds' of up to 95 knots! The engine is not affected by altitude because of its closed-circuit layout and also the system can provide power for high-technology equipment and lighting with the steam generator giving hot water for a variety of uses. Amongst the potential uses for this craft are urban mass transport, anti-submarine patrols, drug trafficking patrols, and timber harvesting.

CHAPTER FIVE

Conclusion

From the perusal of the text of this work it is evident that the use of steam power in aviation was not just a 'flight of fancy', but it was a reality, for two successful attempts were made over a period of 81 years. The first such attempt was made by Henri Giffard on 24 September 1852 when he used a hydrogen-filled dirigible which was fitted with a coal-fired steam plant. He managed to achieve a controlled and sustained flight of some 14 miles at a speed of about 6 mph, being the first person in the history of the world to do so. The other successful attempt took place in the twentieth century when William J. Besler made his epic journey in California on 20 April 1933 using a modified 'Travelair' biplane. Both of these episodes underscored the fact that flight could be achieved using steam as a power source in either the aerostat or aerodyne mode.

Over the years since Sir George Cayley formulated his theories of flight, two methods of approach have been used by the pioneers who, themselves, were divided into two groups. The methods were first scientific, and second 'trial and error'; whilst the two groups of personalities were the 'groundsmen' and the 'airmen'.

Regarding the scientific approach, the activities of Sir Hiram Maxim exemplify this method of attacking the problem during the nineteenth century. Maxim, whilst being an expert craftsman and a good engineer, had one thing in common with others of his genre – he never bothered to investigate what others had achieved or invented before him, and therefore, covered a lot of ground that had already been trodden earlier. The late Dr A.P. Thurston M.B.E., DSc., M.I.Mech.E., F.R.Ae.S. in his Presidential Address to the Newcomen Society which was read at the Science Museum in London on Wednesday, 12 October 1949, told of his father's encouragement of his hobbies of flying machines and kites and of his professional association with Sir Hiram Maxim. Apparently, he was present at Maxim's 'flight' and records it as being on 1 August 1984. However, a note from Lady Maxim written in Sir

Hiram's own copy of his book, *Artificial & Natural Flight*, stated: 'First free flight ever made with a machine heavier than air was made by Sir Hiram Maxim with his large machine on 31 July 1894. This large machine left the ground and engaged the underside of the guide rails and did actually fly a distance of more than 400 ft. This was the first free flight ever made with a machine heavier than air'.

During this incident Sir Hiram was aboard the machine in company with two of his employees, Thomas Jackson and Arthur Coad, and accordingly has been verified and documented. However, the writer considers that it was not a 'free' flight as the machine was constrained by the guide rail system.

Following the scientific theme, Dr Thurston informs us that in 1903 he became Sir Hiram's Chief Assistant and Designer and was involved with the 'whirling-arm' experiments that were conducted at Thurlow Park in Norwood. Unfortunately, Baldwyn's park, the site of the 1894 trials, was sold before Sir Hiram had completed his experiments in 'free flight' and he remarked with some irony at the time: 'I constructed a flying machine weighing 10,000 lb and proved it was possible to lift this weight in the air. The British Government were so pleased that they acquired the site and erected thereon the largest and best equipped lunatic asylum in the world'! This statement revealed two factors about 'flying by steam' – that steam power could, at that time, aerodynamically lift a considerable weight off the ground, and that, also at that time, such experimenters as Sir Hiram Maxim were considered as being completely insane!

Other experimenters during the late nineteenth century also approached the problems of flight using steam engines as their power source, and from a scientific standpoint, did have some degree of success. One of these individuals was Professor Samuel Langley who did achieve some successful results with steam powered models, but unfortunately, failed when attempting to fly full-sized and manned aircraft.

Of 'trial and error', with the emphasis on the latter factor, the saga of Clément Ader was the most pertinent; although Ader was a competent engineer (as shown from the quality of his steam engines), his knowledge of the scientific basis of flight was flawed. For example, several good flying models had been produced in France before his forays into aviation and in 1884, Phillips had already published the results of his work into aerofoils, all of which seem to have been totally disregarded by Ader. For himself, Ader continued with using 'bat-like' wing formations but with single surfaces, and with the use of complex control systems which effected weird and useless wing movement; it was evident that the proliferation of the controls required more hands to operate them than the human being possessed!

All of this was part of a 'trial and error' regime over a period of years. The fact that Clément Ader managed to make the first manned and powered take-off in a heavier than air craft on 9 October 1890 was nothing short of a miracle! Of his 'flights', the September 1891 excursion with the *Éole* at Satory was a fabrication, and the further tests, also at Satory, in the autumn of 1897 with the *Avion III*, were also suspect. The fact that flight was not achieved in 1897 was made clear in the report by Lieutenant General H. Mensier who was the Chairman of the Committee that supervised the tests with the *Avion III*. This report was published on 21 October 1897 and it remained secret for thirteen years until it was officially published in November 1910. Nevertheless, by 1906, Mensier seems to have changed his mind and he implied that others, particularly Lieutenant Binet who was present at the tests, had convinced him that Ader did, indeed, fly and the myth of the 300 metre 'flight' became 'set in the stone of history'.

Later on, in the earlier part of the twentieth century, men like H.H. Groves using a combination of scientific evidence, engineering ability, together with a degree of 'trial and error' did manage to make proper, aerodynamically correct, flights using steam powered models. Full-sized and manned expeditions eluded these pioneers until 20 April 1933 when the 'crowning glory' of steam-powered, heavier than air controlled and sustained manned flight was finally proven when William J. Besler made his epic 90 minute demonstration at San Francisco.

Today, inventors, such as Ronnie Whitehouse, are still at work and could be eminently successful, for with computerised electronic control systems, lightweight airframes made from materials such as Kevlar, titanium, specialised steels and so on, the task is more easily attainable. Indeed, Mr Whitehouse's engine may be picked up in one hand and allied to a light monotube boiler, and it is said to be capable of producing some 90 bhp. This combined with revolutionary 'kit-form' airframes such as the Rutan could make the steam-powered light plane commonplace. If the capital and the foresight are available – then who knows?

Appendix: Artifacts Preserved in Museums

The National Collection, The Science Museum, South Kensington, London

i) Items known to have been deposited in the National Collection from Henson and Stringfellow by C.H. Alderson and P.Y. Alexander unless otherwise specified

INV.NO. 1907-28	Henson and Stringfellow model of 1844/47
INV.NO. 1907-	Eight model airscrews of different types used for thrust tests between 1844 and 1868. No inventory number on computer database
INV.NO. 1908-44	Engine of 1844/47 model
INV.NO. 1908	The engine and boiler of 1848. This was donated by John Heathcote Amory & Co. of Tiverton, Devon, but no inventory number is on the computer database
INV.NO. 1919-552	Listed as 'gliding rail' but possibly the launching apparatus that came with the model of 1848, donated in 1908
INV.NO. 1919	Engine and boiler of the triplane of 1868. Originally on loan from the Royal Aeronautical Society and now possibly returned
INV.NO. 1919	The car, tail, two wings and four propellers from F.J. Stringfellow's model biplane of 1866. Originally on loan from the Royal Aeronautical Society
INV.NO. 1926-560	Replica of the 1848 Stringfellow model (N.B. The original model was donated in 1908 but it was found to have so deteriorated that any reconstruction would have been unsatisfactory.)

ii) Item from Frost ornithopter

INV.NO. 1925-407	Ornithopter wing from 1902

iii) Item from Thomas Moy's experiments

INV.No. 1925-751	Model of Moy's machine, now at Blyth House

iv) Items from the Sir Hiram Maxim Collection

INV.No 1896-98A	Model of Maxim's machine
INV.No 1896-98B	Original engine from Maxim's machine, now at Wroughton Reserve Collection
INV.No 1896-98C	Original 17.83 ft propeller from the Maxim machine, now at Wroughton Reserve Collection
INV.No 1913-429	Ten model propellers, now at Blyth House

INV.No 1922-266	Assortment of struts, wire bracing, fabric covering etc. and a pulley from the original Maxim machine
INV.No 1926-459 & 460	Three 2 ft diameter propellers

In addition to the above there are photographs, letters and documents pertaining to the early pioneers.

The Somerset County Museum, Taunton

i) INV.No 59/2003/1 The Stringfellow airship engine

ii) INV.No 59/2003/2 The boiler for the Stringfellow airship engine

These two items were donated by John Stringfellow's grandaughter, Mrs Marshall in 1940. They were cleaned and conserved by H.C. Stevens of Avimo Ltd, Instrument makers of Taunton, in 1941 and an account of this restoration is given in the Journal of the Somerset Archaeological & Natural History Society, July 1941. There is a box of documents concerning John Stringfellow and Sir Hiram Maxim in the Local Studies Library in Taunton.

The Chard Museum, Chard, Somerset

This museum houses a number of items concerned with the work of Henson and Stringfellow for most of their experiments were conducted in the locality.

i) Model of the 1868 triplane

ii) Model of the 1848 monoplane

iii) Model of a 20 ft wingspan aeroplane made to the patent design

Bilby's Cafe – Chard

The replica of the Stringfellow aeroplane and the engine built by Rolls-Royce apprentices are on display at this location

The Shuttleworth Collection, Old Warden Aerodrome, Dunstable, Bedfordshire

The Frost ornithopter steam engine constructed by Ahrbecker, Son & Hamken of Stamford Street, London, for the 1877 machine is housed here.

The National Collection of the United States of America, The Smithsonian Museum, Washington DC

i)	INV.No 1889-1	The engine constructed by John Stringfellow for the First Aeronautical Exhibition at the Crystal Palace in 1868, purchased by Professor Samuel Pierpoint Langley in 1887 and donated two years later
ii)	INV.No 180.122	Partial reproduction of John Stringfellow's 1868 triplane using some parts of the original reconstructed by Melvin Vaniman and also donated in 1889 by Professor Langley

Museo Nazionale della Scienza e della Technica Leonardo da Vinci, Milan

The Forlanini steam helicopter is in this museum.

Conservatoire des Arts et Métiers, Paris

i) Clément Ader's *Avion III* aircraft of 1897

ii) The steam engine of 20 hp that was made for the *Avion II*

Musée de l'Air, Le Bourget, Paris

The 1879 Tatin compressed air monoplane is housed here.

The House of Aviation (Dom Aviatskaya), Moscow

There is a model of Alexandr Mozhaiskii's aeroplane in this collection but it is conjectural as no accurate illustrations have survived.

Narodni Vekhers Museum, Prague

A small model of Mozhaiskii's aeroplane is to be found in the Aeronautical Gallery.

Bibliography

Books

Ader, Clément, *La Première Étape de l'Aviation Militaire*, Berger-Livrault, Paris/Nancy, 1907–1911 (in French).

Ballantyne, A.M. and Pritchard, J.L., *The Lives and Work of William Samuel Henson and John Stringfellow*, The Journal of the Royal Aeronautical Society, London, 1956.

Benson, J.H. and Rayman, A., *Experimental Flash Steam*, Model & Allied Publications, Hemel Hempstead, 1973.

Brewer, G. and Alexander, P.Y., *Aeronautics: An Abridgement of Aeronautical Specifications filed in the Patent Office from 1815 to 1891*, Patent Office, London, 1893 (Republished in the Netherlands, 1965).

Busgens, G.S., *Aviation in Russia*, Izdatelsvoe Mashinostroenie, Moscow, 1988 (in Russian).

Burton, Robert, *Bird Flight*, Facts on File, New York, 1990.

Chanute, Octave, *Progress in Flying Machines*, the American Engineer & Railroad Journal, New York, 1894.

Davy, M.J.B., *Henson and Stringfellow*, HMSO, London, 1931.

Davy, M.J.B., *Aeronautics: Heavier-Than-Air Aircraft, Parts I and INS*, HMSO, London, 1949.

de Manthé, Georges, *Clément Ader; sa Vie, son Oeuvre*, Paris/Toulouse, 1936.

Dollfus, C. and Bouché, H., *Histoire de L'Aeronautique*, L'Illustration, Paris, 1932 (in French).

Gibbs-Smith, Charles, *The Aeroplane*, HMSO, London, 1960.

Gibbs-Smith, Charles, *Clément Ader: his Flight Claims and his Place in History*, HMSO, London, 1968.

Gibbs-Smith, Charles, *Pioneers of the Aeroplane*, Usbourne Publishing, London, 1975.

Hart, C., *Dream of Flight*, Faber & Faber, London, 1972.

Hart-Davis, Adam, *Eurekaaargh*, Michael O'Mara Books, London, 1999.

Hildebrandt, A., *Airships Past and Present*, Archibald Constable & Co., London, 1908.

Hodgson, J.E., *The History of Aeronautics in Great Britain*, Oxford University Press/ H. Milford, London, 1924.

Hodgson, J.E. (Ed.), *Notebook of Sir George Cayley* c. *1977–1829*, The Newcomen Society (Newcomen Society Extra Publication No. 3), London, 1933.

Jarrett, Phillip, 'Full Marks for Trying', in *Aircraft Annual* (Ed. J.W.R. Taylor), Ian Allan, 1976.

Jarrett, Phillip (Ed.), *Pioneer Aircraft*, Putnam, London, 2002.

John Stringfellow 1799–1883 – Centenary of His Invention of the First Engine Driven Aeroplane, Chard Corporation, Chard, 1948.

John Stringfellow 1799–1883 – The Bi-Centenary of His Birth, Chard Corporation, Chard, 1999.

Langley, Samuel P., *Memoir on Mechanical Flight*, 2 vols., Smithsonian Institute, Washington DC, 1911.

Le Cornu, J., *La Navigation Aerienne*, Viubert et Nony Editeurs, Paris, 1910 (in French).

Maxim, Hiram, *Artificial and Natural Flight*, Whittaker, London, 1908.

Munson, Kenneth, *Pioneer Aircraft 1903-1914*, Blandford Press, London, 1969.

Penrose, Harald, *An Ancient Air*, Airlife Publishing, Shrewsbury, 1998.

Pompien Piraud, J.-C., *Les Secrets du Coup d'Ailes – Essai de Construction d'une Machine Aerienne*, E. Bernard, Paris, 1903 (in French).

Pritchard, J.L., *Sir George Cayley, Bt, The Father of British Aeronautics: the Man and his Work*, The Journal of the Royal Aeronautical Society, London, 1955.

Pritchard, J.L., *Sir George Cayley*, Max Parish, London, 1961.

Randolph, Stella, *Lost Flights of Gustave Whitehead*, Places Inc., Washington DC, 1937.

Shipman, Pat, *Taking Wing – Archaeopteryx and the Revolution of Bird Flight*, Weidenfeld & Nicholson, London, 1998.

Smith, G.G., *Gas Turbines and Jet Propulsion for Aircraft*, 3 eds, Flight, London, 1942–4.

Svoboda, Václav, *Helicopters*, Naše Vojsko, Prague, 1979 (in Czech).

Wright, W. and Wright, O., *The Papers of Wilbur and Orville Wright*, 2 vols, Aeronautics Division of the Library of Congress, New York, 1953.

Magazines, Journals and Newspapers

'The Aviation Problem – A Cambridgeshire Pioneer', *Cambridge Chronicle and University Journal*, 20 September 1912.

Beach, Stanley Y., *Scientific American*, 8 June 1901.

'Birdman's Passion Managed to Get Off the Ground', *Cambridge Evening News*, 4 August 1984.

Breary, F.W., *Popular Science Review*, Vol. VIII, 1869.

Cayley, Sir George, 'On Aerial Navigation', *Nicholson's Journal of Natural Philosophy*, 1809.

Cayley, Sir George, 'Aerial Navigation', *Nicholson's Journal of Natural Philosophy*, 1810.

Cayley, Sir George, 'On Aerial Navigation', *Tillochs Philosophical Magazine*, 1816.

Cayley, Sir George, letter re Pauly and Egg's Delphin Balloon, *Tilloch's Philosophical Magazine*, 1816.

Cayley, Sir George, 'Practical Remarks on Aerial Navigation', *Mechanics Magazine*, 1837.

Cayley, Sir George, 'On the Principles of Aerial Navigation', *Mechanics Magazine*, 6 April 1843.

Cayley, Sir George, 'Governable Parachutes', *Mechanics Magazine*, 25 September 1852.

Cayley, Sir George, 'Memoire sur le Vol Artificiel', *Société Aerostatique et Meteorologique de France Bulletin*, Issue No. 4, 1853.

Clement, Sydney, 'Herreschoff System as Applied to Steam Car Generator', *Steam Car Developments and Steam Marine Motors*, April–September 1948.

Congreve, Sir William, 'A Plan for Raising the Human Body in the Air', *Mechanics Magazine*, 22 March 1828.

'Early Flying in Cambridge – Some attempts and Some Achievements', *Cambridge Independent Press*, 5 July 1929.

'An Early Flying Machine – A Chat with a Cambridgeshire Pioneer', *Cambridge Weekly News*, 23 August 1918.

'A Fine Old English Gentleman – Death of the Squire of West Wratting', *Cambridge Chronicle and University Journal*, 1 February 1922.

'Flying', *Bridgeport Herald*, 18 August 1901.

'Full Steam Ahead for World Record', *Hampstead Advertiser*, 1 February 1990.

Groves, H.H., 'Steam plant for Model Aeroplanes', *Model Engineer*, May 1913.
Hawkins, E. Caesar, 'Aeronautical Notes', *The Autocar*, 14 July 1906.
Thurston, Dr A.P., 'Reminiscences of Early Aviation', excerpt from Presidential Address. *Transactions of the Newcomen Society*, Vol. xxvii, 1949–50 and 1950–1
Jarrett, Phillip, 'Claims to Fame, Alexandr Mozhaiskii', *The Aeroplane*, January 2003.
Light Steam Power, various items from 1951 to 1964.
'L.L.', 'The Aerial Steam Carriage', *Mechanics Magazine*, 1 April 1843.
'Revolutionary Engine Faces Apathy Barrier', *Ham & High*, 1 February 1990.
Rosser, Nigel, 'The Magnificent "Green" Machine', *Evening Standard*, 11 January 1990.
Stevens, George, 'Steam Aircraft', *Old Motor*, April 1967.
Stokes, P.R., 'Powered Flight: A Russian Backwater', *Transactions of the Newcomen Society*, Vol. 63, 1991–1992.
Wenham F.H., 'Aerial Locomotion', paper read to the Society of Arts, 27 June 1866.
Wright, Orville, *US Air Services Magazine*, August 1945.

Index